THEOLOGY OF LIMITS AND THE LIMITS OF THEOLOGY

Reflections on Language, Environment and Death

Hugh T. McElwain

UNIVERSITY
PRESS OF
AMERICA

LANHAM • NEW YORK • LONDON

Copyright © 1983 by

University Press of America,™ Inc.

4720 Boston Way
Lanham, MD 20706

3 Henrietta Street
. London, WC2E 8LU England

ISBN (Perfect): 0-8191-3094-X
ISBN   (Cloth): 0-8191-3093-1

To Anne for her constant support, from patient understanding and listening to proofreading;

To Seán, Brian and Karen Anne who perhaps taught me
most about limits and about transcendence.

ACKNOWLEDGEMENTS

"Measure" and from "Saliences" in DIVERSIFICATIONS:
POEMS by A. R. Ammons. Copyright © 1975 by A. R.
Ammons. Reprinted by permission of W. W. Norton & Co.,
Inc.

"Meeting the Opposition" and from "One: Many" in THE
SELECTED POEMS: 1951-77 by A. R. Ammons. Copyright ©
1977, 1975, 1974, 1972, 1971, 1970, 1966, 1965, 1964,
1955 by A. R. Ammons. Reprinted by permission of W. W.
Norton & Co., Inc.

From THE GOLD OF THE TIGERS by Jorge Luis Borges, translated by Alastair Reid. English translation Copyright
© 1976, 1977 by Alastair Reid. Reprinted by permission
of the publisher, E. P. Dutton, Inc.

From DREAMTIGERS by Jorge Luis Borges. Copyright ©
1964 by Jorge Luis Borges. Reprinted by permission of
University of Texas Press, Austin, Texas.

From "East Coker" in THE FOUR QUARTETS, copyright 1943
by T. S. Eliot; renewed 1971 by Esme Valerie Eliot. Reprinted by permission of Harcourt Brace Jovanovich, Inc.

From "De Rerum Virtute," "Carmel Point," and "Beauty of
Things" in HUNGERFIELD AND OTHER POEMS by Robinson Jef-
fers. Copyright © 1951, 1952, 1954 by Robinson Jeffers.
Reprinted by permission of the publisher Random House,
Inc.

From "Go Down Death" from GOD'S TROMBONES by James Weldon Johnson. Copyright 1927 by The Viking Press, Inc.
Copyright renewed 1955 by Grace Nail Johnson. Reprinted
by permission of Viking Penguin, Inc.

"Bus" from THE FREEZING OF THE DUST by Denise Levertov.
Copyright © 1975 by Denise Levertov. Reprinted by permission of New Directions Publishing Corporation.

From "Deathmother" in DEATHMOTHER AND OTHER POEMS by
Frederick Morgan. Copyright © 1979 by Frederick Morgan.
Reprinted by permission of the University of Illinois
Press.

From "Canto LXXXI" and "Canto LXXXVI." Ezra Pound, THE
CANTOS OF EZRA POUND. Copyright © 1948, 1956 by Ezra
Pound. Reprinted by permission of New Directions
Publishing Corporation.

TABLE OF CONTENTS

PREFACE

Amidst a plethora of contemporary theologies, liberation, political, dialectical, process, contextual, and others, I have been particularly taken by the theology of story. That theology seemed to me to be the most realistic and helpful in the fundamental task of bringing together religion as institutional experience and religion as personal story. Teaching religious studies on college campuses for the past two decades, I have found that the transition for students from personal story to institutional experience and vice versa is difficult and often painful. The theology of story, or approaching religion as story, furnished me with a model which enabled me to deal more directly with that transition.

Yet, there was, I sensed, a void in the theology of story. The precise problem most often was with the traditional story itself, especially its seeming inadequacy and/or irrelevance in view of contemporary experiences and changing world views. The challenge was to point out in the very context of story the inherent fact of limits. And so grew gradually the notion of limits as a dimension of the theology of story. More forcefully stated, essential to the constructive and myth-making dimension of story is the de-constructive and parabolic dimension of story. This essay is an attempt to demonstrate the particular relationship between the theology of story and the theology of limits.

I am deeply indebted to several colleagues and dear friends for the gradual maturing of these reflections, especially to J. Dominic Crossan whose influence will be obvious to anybody familiar with his work in this area, and to Charles Strain whose insights and encouragement were so thoughtfully offered. I am also grateful to my colleagues in Religious Studies at Rosary College who picked up the slack while I retreated for six months to pull together these ideas. Finally, I would like to thank Mrs. Judy Davies for typing the final draft of the manuscript and assisting in earlier drafts.

Rosary College
December, 1982

Introduction

At precisely that point in history when humanity has reached its zenith in technological expertise and electronic control, a gnawing awareness of limitation and constraint begins to surface. Limits to resources, limits to population, and limits to growth generally, arrive as the unwelcome guests at the celebration of technological utopia.

These reflections on the theology of 'limit', as well as being an exercise in philosophical theology pointing toward a clarification and a particular characterization of religious and theological language as limit-language, are also a commentary on the frustration and disappointment of the (Western) technological community of this last quarter of the twentieth century. Seeing the reigning monarchs of the land(s) of limitless possibility squirming in the face of the inevitable prospects of scarcity and restriction, one cannot help but think of the original Prometheus bound to the rock--not, indeed, because of anything "wrong," but rather because he overstepped his 'limits'. It is not a question so much of punishment as of the consequences of action. If we are to learn from history (indeed, we may not be fortunate enough to be 'doomed' to repeat it), perhaps the motto of the coming generation will be "living within limits."

The thrust and direction of this study is that language (story) creates the world, and that therefore the story (myth) we tell creates and defines the world we live in. An obvious conclusion from this premise is that the appropriate (adequate, right, proper) story is essential.[1] And yet even the "right" story necessarily requires a self-consciously critical appropriation of it, since it also is our creation and thus subject to the limits and boundaries of our time and place and our culture generally. It is the function of a theology of limit to suggest both that every story be consciously autocritical and also that each generation be conscious of critically appropriating and telling (or re-telling) its story.

In the analysis of the nature and function of the theology of limit, we rely primarily on the experience of limit, especially as that is realized in the limits of language (the limit that is language), the ecologic limits (the limit that is environment), and the limits

1

of death (the limit that _is_ death). These three contexts of limit will be preceded by an analysis of the
notion of limit itself and followed by an evaluative
summary of the theology of limit.

CHAPTER I

LIMITS

Studies relating to the question of 'limits' have become fashionable of late.[1] We might suspect that reflection on 'limit', coming as it does at this point in human history, is no accident. The conjunction of ecological constraint, and international political tensions in the context of nuclear armaments on the one hand, and a deep awareness of human limits on the other, makes good sense in the last two decades of our century.

Daedalus, the prestigious journal of the American Academy of Arts and Sciences, has devoted two of its past half-dozen or so issues to aspects of the question of 'limit'.[2] Choice had as a lead article in a recent issue a general discussion of bibliography about the human predicament (aspects of which referred to the question of 'limits').[3] The watershed for much of this reflection was the study from the Club of Rome titled precisely, Limits to Growth.[4] Moving to more specific areas within the question of 'limits', Garrett Hardin, somewhat leery of the utopian aspects of altruism, cautioned in trenchant terms about its 'limits'.[5] Coming finally to works more directly related to theological discourse, I have found invaluable assistance in several authors who have wrestled with the meaning and implications of 'limit' for religious studies and theology. John D. Crossan's In Parables and The Dark Interval are ground-breaking and seminal studies in the literary and biblical presuppositions of any theology of limit.[6] David Tracy's Blessed Rage for Order addresses directly the issue of religious and theological language as limit-language.[7] Paul Van Buren's The Edges of Languages was one of the early efforts to systematically explore the relationship between 'edges' and 'limits' of language generally and its implications for religious and, particularly, Christian religious discourse.[8] Finally, one cannot ignore Paul Ricoeur's immeasurable contribution to the analysis of religious language as "going to the limit" and "limit-expressions."[9]

The emergence of 'limit' as a significant characteristic of religious and theological language in my own thinking coincided with research over a decade ago (for an undergraduate course) on death and afterlife in religious thought.[10] About the same time, I began

3

to work out a college course on religion and ecology, when the publication of The Limits of Growth suggested a logical expansion of the category of 'limit' to ecology.[11] Further reflection on the category of limit as applicable both to religious reflections on death (existential challenge of ultimacy) and to religious reflections on ecology (environmental 'crisis') led eventually to a research paper presented to the American Academy of Religion.[12]

The final--and indeed pivotal--step in my own reflections on the theology of limit was the incorporation of language as the third member of the trinity of limits.[13] Thus my reflections had been expanded to embrace the religious experience of and discourse about the limits of language, environment, and death. More research on the limits of language, ecologic limits, and the limits of death, and on the reality of 'limit' itself, led to another paper presented also to the American Academy of Religion.[14] This is a chronological account, of course.

My approach here will be more logical. I will begin with the general notion of 'limit'. Then I will move seriatim to the limits of language, religious language as limit-language and, finally, theology of limit.

1. DEFINITION OF LIMIT

If it were a question simply of describing the word, 'limit', a sentence perhaps would be adequate (for example, a limit is whatever cuts something off, bounds or circumscribes it). Such, however, is not the case, even though any effort to demonstrate why would take us into the central thrust of this study, namely, the distinction between limit as limitation (boundary, constraint, restriction)[15] and limit as presupposition (ground, possibility, horizon).[16] Failure to take into account this distinction between limit as limitation (negative connotation) and limit as possibility seems to characterize much contemporary discussion of 'limit'.[17] I think it fair to say that the enigma facing 20th-century humanity derives in no small part from the contrast, not between limit as constraint and limit as horizon, but rather between limited and limitless. Contemporary technological man (homo technicus) reads reality in terms of barriers to be "broken," frontiers to be "settled," and space to be "conquered." Human possibilities must be limit-

4

less, for to be limit-ed is to some extent to be controlled, but homo technicus shall not be controlled.
Indeed, he controls![18]

Back, then, to the description or definition of
limit. The suggested ambiguity of defining limit,
that is, the ordinary dictionary definition versus the
qualified description, points up perhaps the central
thrust of my whole approach to 'limit'. We shall say,
then, by way of an opening summary, that limit in
ordinary language is generally taken to mean limitation, restriction, constraint, or barrier, all of
which refer to the limiting or restricting dimension.
In a somewhat more reflective and qualified sense,
however, limit is defined also as ground, horizon,
possibility, presupposition.[19] In other words, the
question about 'limit' is not only of limitation and
boundaries, but also about whether such boundaries are
solely restrictive (limiting), or creative as well,
that is, liberating and challenging.[20] This was the
sense of 'limit' that was explored by the Daedalus
proceedings:

>...But which of these limits (to intel-
>lectual inquiry) ... are real epistemo-
>logical barriers beyond which sentient
>man cannot pass, and which are merely
>stumbling blocks of our own making, the
>products of ignorance, fear, or prejudg-
>ment? Can we change limits from re-
>strictive boundaries to creative possi-
>bilities? How does the intellect sur-
>pass limits and in so doing redefine
>them?[21]

It is this basic theme of limit both as "restrictive
boundary" and "creative possibility" which weaves in
and out of my reflections on limit in general and also
on the theology of limit.

Before we leave the definition of limit, it might
be enlightening to dwell briefly on the question of
the source of limits. Although we will want to say
that the comprehensive and over-arching source for
limits is the very nature of language and stories,[22]
perhaps it will be helpful here to examine another approach that locates 'limits' within the context of biological and cultural constraints.[23] The difficulty one
runs into in the interface between biology and culture
in the question of limits is a difficulty that we will

have to face throughout these pages, namely, that somehow science, dealing with "objective reality," wants
to be exempt from the limitation of language and story.
We will address this question directly in a later
section,[24] but for now two observations need to be
shared: First, one cannot assume privileged status
for any particular way of knowing, whether scientific,
philosophical, or religious, since all of these approaches have their own stories of our being-in-the-
world-with-others. In other words, all of the stories
are relational and relative, since there is no "objective reality" against which all stories can be measured, nor--which is to say the same thing--does anyone
possess the master-story that may serve as the measure
for all others.[25]

The second observation is related to the first.
The position taken above is not only contrary to what
we have been accustomed to assume about "reality," but
it is even more disconcerting since it challenges the
secure, reliable, "real" world on which we have come
to depend.[26] The point I am making is that there is
no quarrel with the variety of stories (ideologies).[27]
What is disputed, rather, is the claim of any one to
absolute and objective status.

Let us attempt now to draw some conclusions about
the general notion of limit. First, the definition or
description of 'limits' in everyday usage conveys the
sense of limitation, restriction and constraint.
Limits are seen as barriers. They become, especially
for homo technicus, manacles, shackles, and controls
to be thrown off or broken. It is for this reason
that the two comprehensive contexts of human life,
namely, environment and death, especially, have become,
almost unconsciously for modern humanity, major
problems. The problematic impact of the realities of
ecology and death, however, is felt more in their
avoidance than in any confrontation and resolution. I
mean particularly the reluctance of contemporary
humanity to acknowledge the finiteness (limits) of our
eco-system, on the one hand, and our unwillingness, on
the other hand, or inability, to face the reality of
death, the abiding symbol of human finitude and mortality. Add to these, finally, the virtually impossible task of realizing the import of language and its
limits (in story), and one sees the three major dimensions of the experience of limit.[28]

Language in fact is so intertwined with the human

6

experience that we find it impossible to determine a vantage point from which to discuss language (since one would be using language and thus prejudicing one's analysis). Language to man is like water to a fish, or, to quote Van Buren's analogy:

> An investigation of words and our language, however, places us in a circular situation: the very language in which the problem is presented is also the only tool we have for solving it. This means we are in a position like that of a man who wishes to examine the lenses of his eyes, yet must have those lenses in place in order to carry out his examination....[29]

The upshot of all of this is that we so take language for granted that we fail to realize its limits, that is, that it is <u>our</u> creation by which <u>we</u> define world and then live in <u>it</u> like a spider in <u>his</u> web, to use Geertz's analogy.[30] This failure leads again to a kind of general assumption within the culture--indeed, pervading our culture's very fabric--that the only reliable and trustworthy discourse is that provided by factual, verifiable, that is, scientific language. Language in this perspective effectively is limited to the real world "out there"--hard, factual, sense data. Beyond this there is either fantasy (in all of its various forms) or nonsense.[31]

Once again the sense of limit as applied to language connotes limitation, barriers, confines. Linguistic flexibility, whether of philosophy, poetry, religion, etc., is seen as valid only when measured by the "real" world--the given (factual, measurable, quantifiable reality). This approach is quite well defined: language describes the objective, existing, manageable world (reality) out there. Language therefore is limited "responsibly" to the facts, to the real world. To push at the edges, limits and borders of language (reality) is effectively to lapse into nonsense. More and more, one has the distinct impression that words have lost out to numbers in our time.[32]

Perhaps one final note is in order regarding the general notion of limits, and it deals with our horse-cart problem, that is, the inevitable intertwining between the general question of limit and the experience of limit through language, environment and death. On

7

the one hand, the inevitable experience of limits is within and through language, ecology, and death. At the same time, it seems wise to flesh-out the abstract notion of limit to some extent, so that the import of the ongoing reflections on the experience of limit will be sufficiently seen.

With this cursory examination of the notion of limits completed, then, we will pass on to the particular contexts within which limit is most authentically experienced, namely, language, environment, and death.

INTRODUCTION AND CHAPTER I NOTES

Introduction:

1. This is said here and throughout this essay under
   the assumption that there is no master-story--at
   least that we know. Perhaps the central element
   in Faith is precisely commitment without knowing
   the whole story, or, as it were, "having the big
   picture."

Chapter I

1. Following are just a random sampling of titles from
   a college library card catalogue: Jonathan
   Benthali (Ed.), The Limits of Human Nature (New
   York: Dutton, 1974); David Granvogel, Limits of
   the Novel (Ithaca, New York: Cornell U. Press,
   1968); James L. Guetti, The Limits of Metaphor
   (Ithaca, Cornell U. Press, 1967); Robert Heil-
   broner, The Limits of American Capitalism (New
   York: Harper & Row, 1966); Peter Marin (Ed.), The
   Limits of Schooling (Englewood Cliffs, N.J.:
   Prentice-Hall, 1975); Eugene McCarthy, The Limits
   of Power (New York: Holt, Rinehart & Winston,
   1967); Normal Miller, Limits: The Concept and its
   Role in Mathematics (New York: Blaisdell, 1964);
   Paul Ramsey, The Limits to Nuclear War (New York:
   CRIA, 1963); Andrew Tolson, The Limits of Masculin-
   ity (New York: Harper & Row, 1979); Bernard Wein-
   berg, The Limits of Symbolism (Chicago: University
   of Chicago Press, 1966).
       An interesting observation about all these
   essays is that, except for Normal Miller's (Limits:
   The Concept and its Role in Mathematics), not one
   of them deals with the concept of limit directly.
   All make assumptions about its meaning, and that
   generally is limit-as-restriction or limitation.

2. Daedalus, 107: 1978 and 109:1980

3. Choice, 87:1980, pp. 181-194

4. Donella Meadows, etal. The Limits to Growth (New
   York: Universe, 1972).

5. Garrett Hardin, The Limits of Altruism (Blooming-
   ton, IN: University of Indiana Press, 1977).

6. John Dominic Crossan, _The Dark Interval_ (Niles, IL: Argus Communications, 1975).

7. David Tracy, _Blessed Rage for Order_ (New York: Seabury, 1975). We will be using also a revision of chapters four and five of this work, contained in an article by David Tracy, "Religious Language as Limit-language," _Theology Digest_ 22: 1973, pp. 291-307.

8. Paul Van Buren, _The Edges of Language_ (New York: Macmillan, 1972).

9. Paul Ricoeur, _Semeia_ 4: 1975, pp. 29-148.

10. James W. Van Evra, "On Death as a Limit," _Analysis_ 31: 1971, pp. 170-176, and a critical response in A. C. Genova, "Death as a _Terminus ad quem_," _Philosophy & Phenomenological Research_ 34: 1973, pp. 270-77.

11. Donella Meadows, _Limits to Growth_.

12. "Religion and Ecology: The Issue is Limits," delivered at the Midwest Regional Meeting of the American Academy of Religion, Adrian College, Adrian, Michigan, 1976.

13. Extended conversations with my friend, John Dominic Crossan, led to some initial probings to incorporate language and limits into the already existing context.

14. "Language, Environment, and Death: Religion and the Experience of Limit," delivered to the Section on Religious Reflection, the Annual Meeting of the American Academy of Religion, New York, 1979.

15. In the preface to the _Daedalus_ issue cited above (109: 1980), we read
    The words 'intellect and imagination' have a fine resonance; taken alone their timbre is at once self-confident and assertive; they are clearly universal goods. Add to this, however, the subscription 'the limits and pre-suppositions of intellectual inquiry,' and the mood changes--a beguiling concept that seemed to soar, without _impediment_ or _control_ becomes

somewhat flattened, shackled, inhibited,
constricted... (p.v.)

16. The Daedalus article just cited continued:
...Yet both phrases are necessary for a faithful rendering of the context (of this issue on
limits)...It is more than the merely contemporary preoccupation with the idea of 'limits'
increasingly fashionable in so many quarters...
It is an argument for a more self-conscious
probing of the condition that governs our in-
tellectual lives. (p.v.)
This distinction between the negative connotation
of limit, and its positive dimension will for now
generally be described as 'limiting' and
'grounding'. Later on we will examine and sub-
sequently adopt David Tracy's terminology of
'limit-to' (limiting limitation) and 'limit-of'
(grounding, disclosing).

17. One could choose as examples virtually any of the
essays cited above (p. 3, n. 1).

18. As William Barrett writes poignantly, "... Nature
sinks to the level of mere material for exploitation, and man towers as the master over it..."
The Illusion of Technique (Garden City, NY:
Anchor Press/Doubleday, 1978), p. 191-2.

19. In this sense, creativity has become the key term.
See, for example, Meredith Skura, "Creativity:
Transgressing the Limits of Consciousness,"
Daedalus 109: 1980, pp. 127-146.

20. Rollo May in The Courage to Create (New York: W.
W. Norton, 1975) has an informative chapter en-
titled, "On the Limits of Creativity."

21. Daedalus 109: 1980, p. vii.

22. See ahead in this essay, pp. 17ff.

23. See Stephen J. Gould, "The Evolutionary Biology
of Constraint," Daedalus 109: 1980, pp. 39-52.

24. In the section on "Story and Limit," and especially "Theology of Story."

25. We have already made reference to this point (p.
2, n.1). It seems important, however, to dis-

11

tinguish between there being a "master-story,"
and someone's possessing it. We are certain
only about the latter assertion, viz., that
nobody possesses the story.

26. Cf. the following analysis by Michael Noval in
his Ascent of the Mountain, Flight of the Dove
(New York: Harper & Row, 1978):
...One can criticize the story a person
chooses to live out (i.e., "Nazi Storm
Trooper") on many grounds. The Nazi who
prided himself on living out the Nazi
story to perfection was, in a limited
sense of the word, a "good" Nazi. But in
a moral sense of the word, the story he
chose to live out was murderous, bar-
barous, and destructive. What he did was
wrong because his story, judged against
other human stories, was wrong (pp. 70f.)

27. See Crossan's comment in The Dark Interval:
The most basic question for a theology of
limit and of story is whether there is any
such direct, ordinary, objective, descriptive language as over against some other
type... To concede objectivity to scientific
language is to lose the battle before the
first shot is fired... (p. 26).

28. The discussion of the 'limits of language',
however, as we shall note often, is different
in degree and in kind from the other experiences
of limit. The limits of language, as we shall
attempt to show, become the matrix and the context for the other experiences of limit.

29. Paul Van Buren, The Edges of Language, p. 45.

30. Clifford Geertz, The Interpretation of Culture
(New York: Basic Books, 1973), p. 5.

31. We will be examining much more closely in the
next section the relationship between language
and reality; this deference to the priority of
scientific language will be seriously challenged.

32. See John Hersey, "Science and/or Humanities: The
Triumph of Number," Current, Dec., 1980, pp. 21-
33. Also Huston Smith in his The Forgotten Truth
(New York: Harper & Row, 1976) makes the same

point with an interesting anecdote:

    ... I found myself seated next to a scientist,
and as so often happened in such circumstances
the conversation turned to the difference between science and the humanities. We were
getting nowhere when suddenly he broke in on
something I was saying with the authority of a
man who has discovered Truth. "I have it!" he
exclaimed. "The difference between us is that
I count and you don't." The key differences
between the primordial and contemporary perspectives in a double entendre. (p. 11, n.11)

CHAPTER II

LANGUAGE AND THE EXPERIENCE OF LIMIT

> To say more than human things with
>   human voice,
> That cannot be; to say human things
>   with more
> than human voice, that, also, cannot be;
> To speak humanly from the height or
>   from the depth
> Of human things, that is acutest speech.
>
> --Wallace Stevens, Chocorua
>   to its Neighbor, XXX[1]

A passing glance at the format of this study might
suggest that the relationship between language and
limit is simply one of three authentic modes of experiencing limit, along with environment and death.
Such a conclusion would be unacceptable. The limits
of language (the limit which language is) portray a
particularly central and paradigmatic experience of
limit. In fact, the limits of language determine the
context within which the other two parts of this essay
are situated. The limits of environment and the
limits of death are discussed obviously (and necessarily) in language. The issues of limit and language, therefore, are tutorial to any further discussion of limits, whether of environment or death.
Mapping the vast terrain suggested by a study of the
limits of language, we might highlight several distinct features which will serve as signposts for our
reflections: 1) Language and reality; 2) Religious
language and the theology of limit; 3) Limits of
language as the context for further discussion.

1. LANGUAGE AND REALITY

A section in any book on "language and reality"
brings to mind the adage: "On Every Knowable Thing."[2]
The ramifications of this question about language and
reality are indeed extensive, covering philosophical
development roughly from Kant through Wittgenstein into the positivists and, finally, ending with the linguistic analysts.[3] Our intention here is to keep this
development constantly before us, especially the significant place of Wittgenstein in the whole process of
the philosophy of religious language.[4] More exactly,
our investigation will proceed along three main lines:

i.   Language and world; ii. Language and story;   iii.
Story and limit.

i.   Language and world. The following quote sets the
tone for our discussion of language and reality-world:

> Interest in language is not new, but the
> increasing intensity of concern with which
> man reflects upon language is new. The
> interest is tightly woven into the intri-
> cate design of our contemporary scene; the
> fabric of our age is to a large extent lan-
> guage textured...[5]

The two persons perhaps most responsible for the
tonality and tenor of this discussion are Ludwig
Wittgenstein and Martin Heidegger.[6]

The relationship between language and world is
keyed clearly and directly by Wittgenstein in his
famous quote from the Tractatus: " ... the limits of
my language mean the limits of my world."[7] The world
around me is the world of my language. Wittgenstein
continues:

> Logic pervades the world: the limits of
> the world are also its limits...
>   The world is my world: this is manifest
> in the fact that the limits of language
> (of that language which alone I under-
> stand) mean the limits of my world. The
> world and life are one.[8]

Heidegger is equally direct in his analysis of the
limits of language: "Only where there is language is
there world..."[9] And Seffler comments on Heidegger's
insight:

> Heidegger likewise maintains that language
> is the limit of the world. It is language
> which structures and differentiates things
> of the world. For, it is only language
> that creates the very possibility of
> standing in the overtness of existence,
> Heidegger remarks. Language is the arti-
> culating creation of the world; it de-
> marcates and delineates the world...[10]

The sense of both Wittgenstein's and Heidegger's reflections is unambiguous: language creates world.

16

Language does not merely point to my world, as we so naturally assume (picture-theory of reality), but actually brings it about.[11] What is demanded, given the validity of these statements about language, is a radical reassessment of the relationship between language and reality, that is, language and world.

This is a challenge of some consequence, since, as we suggested earlier,[12] language so surrounds our being that we can find no point of perspective outside of it. As Wittgenstein asserts, "What expresses it-self in language we cannot express by means of language."[13] The fish and water analogy, as well as the lenses-and-eyes comparison, are helpful here. The latter is Van Buren's example:

> ... we are in a position like that of a man who wishes to examine the lenses of his eyes, yet must have these lenses in place in order to carry out his examination. Nor is there any way out of this circle: words are so centrally and inextricably a part of our life that there is no Archimedean point from which the puzzle can be unraveled...[14]

The measure of the task before us lies in our ability to realize that we humans create the world in which we live by our language (story) about it and about us in it. To quote Van Buren once more, "... with language we fashion (or accept from others) the world about us. The only world we have is the one we can speak of.[15] The world is ours therefore as we speak of it... " Any theory therefore about humankind must begin with the primary reality about man, that is, language and story.[16] The key word here is story, and that leads into the next issue of concern.

ii. _Language and story_. The transition in our reflections from language and world to language and story is not quite as abrupt as it may first appear. Such assertions as: language creates world, the limits of my language are the limits of my world, and similar statements all lead to the centrality in human history of storytelling and mythmaking. Story and myth, in other words, are simply language in action.[17] Language as an intersubjective and relational activity--the sense in which we are using the term here--is the (a) story about ourselves and our world. The obvious conclusion is that humans tell stories (and make myths) as part

17

and parcel of their being (-in-the-world).

There is nothing new or novel about this fact. Anthropologists, literary critics, and philosophers and historians of religions, amongst others from the community of scholars, have endlessly analyzed and synthesized the heritage of stories (and myths) from the human community. Northrop Frye's classification of the archetypes of myth is perhaps the classical summation of this vast heritage.[18] One critical question, however, must be raised in this important study of man the storyteller (and mythmaker):

> Is story telling us about a world out there objectively present before and apart from any story concerning it, or, does story create world so that we live as human beings in, and only in, layers of interwoven story?[19]

The answer to this question is already contained, at least implicitly, in what has been discussed earlier in the interface between language and world. But the question needs to be highlighted, since it focuses the relationship between language and story. We are already living a story--as humans--before we begin to become (self-) conscious of it and to reflect upon it. It has already given us-in-our-world firm form and definition before we begin any critical appropriation. This is a fundamental thrust of the genre of story.

A final point on the issue of language and story will be necessary to enable us to make the transition to the question of story and limit, our next concern. Story may have various modes or forms, as we discussed earlier,[20] but the central issue here is that, since (our) story creates (our) world (or explains, justifies, criticizes or subverts it), we are led inevitably to the limits of living within that story-world. And that takes us directly into the third and concluding point of this chapter.

iii. Story and limit. In the context of the foregoing discussion, the relationship between story and limit ought to be coming gradually into focus. Progressively our investigations have moved from language and limits to the relationship between language and story, and logically to the limits of story. To repeat our analogies one more time, the fish is unaware of water--

until there is none; the eye is unaware of lens--until it is gone. Similarly, we are unaware of our language-story (as about anything but the real world) until it is subverted and shattered.[21] It is in the disintegration of myth that we recognize relativity, limitation, and (even) possibility. We might presume to re-interpret the famous quote from Wittgenstein cited earlier as follows: the limits of my _story_ mean the limits of my world. The world is _my_ world. This is manifest in the fact that the limits of _story_ (of that _story_ which alone I understand) mean the limits of _my_ world. The world and life are one.[22]

The point is, in fact, that we are always living a story, before we become reflectively aware of it, and indeed _even if_ we do not initiate this painful process of self-conscious criticism of our story. As Crossan notes: "We are involved in the inevitable limits of living within story. It may be _this_ story or _another_ story, but it is always story."[23] It is this fact that underlies the circularity regarding language and story about which Van Buren spoke earlier.[24]

Perhaps we are in a position now to draw some con-clusions about language and reality, the subject-matter of this section. First, it seems clear from our analysis that humans construct reality for themselves insofar as they tell stories about themselves-in-their-world, and then they are "constrained" to live within the limits of their stories and their worlds. There is, however, a tendency to push at the limits and edges of one's story, either because experience cannot be contained within it, or because (poetic) creativity imagines different stories about world and self, and indeed--sometimes in patent revolutionary fashion-- creates new worlds. It is precisely these experiences, or at least the _possibility_ of such experiences, that undergird the theology of limit.

2. RELIGIOUS LANGUAGE AND THEOLOGY OF LIMIT

The critical transition point in this study is centered here in the passage from the limits of lan-guage to the theology of limit. Exploring this passage will lead us into four distinct areas: i. Limits of language and religious language; ll. Limiting and grounding dimensions of religious language; iii. Limit and transcendence; iv. Theology of story and theology of limit.

i. <u>Limits of language and religious language</u>. We
might open up this section with a brief, summary statement: Religion is linguistic behavior (sometimes ex-
pressly so with scriptures, creeds, etc., and sometimes not so obvious as with symbol, ritual, etc.), and
so, at least implicitly, everything we have predicated
about language and limits would be applicable to
religious language. At the same time, however, this
general principle does not represent the many dimensions of religious language and the question of limits.
We will speak, therefore, directly to the notion of
religious and theological language as limit-language.
I will be following very closely the direction indi-
cated by David Tracy.[25]

The first point to note is that all religious
language (as linguistic behavior) is limit-language.
Several qualifications must be added, however: first,
not <u>only</u> religious language manifests the particular
characteristics of limit-language (other modes of discourse exhibit similar characteristics, e.g., poetry
and paradox); and second, limit is "offered as <u>a</u>
defining characteristic disclosive of the autonomy of
religious and theological language, not a universal
definition of 'religion' .... further characteristics
implied by the traditions of <u>analogical</u> and <u>dialecti-</u>
<u>cal</u> analyses clearly imply other characteristics of
that language... "[26]

Perhaps we ought to pause here momentarily to
clear up any confusion resulting from the variety of
ways in which religious and theological language is
being described as limit-language. The direction
taken by Van Buren, following Wittgenstein, is to talk
about linguistic behavior, religious language being a
particular form or expression of such behavior. Thus
when Van Buren talks about religious language, he is
speaking about a particular kind of linguistic behavior, namely, at the "edges of language." His point
is that linguistic behavior at the center of language
is readily grasped and approximates what one might
call the factual, the readily sayable. Following is
his own analysis:

> Using this picture (language as a plat-
> form rather than a cage), we may speak
> of the edges of language rather than of
> its limits. We can go so far out on
> the platform of language, but if we try
> to go further, we fall off into a mis-

> use of words, into nonsensical jab-
> bering, into the void where rules
> give out. We can, if we are so in-
> clined, walk right along the edges
> of language .... We can, on the
> other hand, find this a silly place
> to stand and choose to confine our
> life to the no-nonsense areas as
> well within the edges of language,
> where the rules are clear, their ap-
> plication is undisputed, and language
> is safely unproblematic.[27]

Van Buren's approach would appear to approximate a
final Wittgensteinian position, that is, partly from
the _Tractatus_, and partly from the _Investigations_. In
other words, to paraphrase Wittgenstein's interpreters,
language games are more or less intelligible the more
they approximate ordinary usage of language, the range
going from the expressable (factual) to the transcendental or ineffable (religious). Limits therefore can
be easily described as edges, and religious linguistic
behavior as less 'reliable', 'more risky', ambiguous,
etc., because walking at (and teetering on) the edges
of language.[28]

Following Van Buren's approach, however, one is
led to the possible conclusion that religious language
is just another of·the language games. This not only
has its problems as an adequate interpretation of
Wittgenstein,[29] but also differs in some ways from the
manner in which Tracy and Ricoeur use the concept of
limit-language.[30] It is this difference that interests
me now and which also forms the context for the next
question.

ii. _Religious language as limiting (limit-to) and_
grounding (limit-of). In the earlier discussions on
limit in general, we underscored several times the
distinction between 'limit' as _limiting_, restricting,
etc., and 'limit' as _grounding_, expanding (possibility,
horizon, presupposition), and so forth. The same
basic distinction is proffered by Tracy, but with the
particular nuances proper to religious language:

> .... The word 'limit' here will in-
> volve two interrelated notions: first,
> religious language as a limit-to our
> more ordinary modes of discourse and
> experience (the everyday, the

21

scientific, the moral, and aesthetic,
the political) and, by way of that
autonomous 'limit-to' character,
religious language functions as an
authentic disclosure--a 'showing'
though rarely a 'stating'--of a final
grounding--even an ultimate-dimension
to our lives: in that sense religious
language is also a 'limit-of' language
as well.[31]

Tracy's distinction then between religious language as
having both a limit-to and a limit-of character seems
to very nearly parallel the earlier notion of limit
itself as simultaneously limiting (limit-to) and
grounding (limit-of). There are significant differences, however, and they need to be emphasized.

Tracy himself notes that the "limit character of
religious and theological language must be analyzed in
both 'limit questions' and 'limit situations' present
in our common human experience and in the explicit
limit-expressions of the 'religions'.[32] The implications of this statement are complex and must be carefully unpacked. As far back as Stephen Toulmin's
adoption of the term, the notion of 'limiting
question' as one requiring a properly religious response has been discussed among philosophers of
religion.[33] In a recent article, Kai Nielsen provides
an interesting summary of the discussion regarding
'limiting questions'.[34] He is responding to and
criticizing an earlier article by Robert Coburn.[35] It
will be very helpful here to review the Coburn-Nielsen
exchange.

Coburn begins by interpreting the category of
'limiting questions' as a distinctive type of question
which religious utterances "normally function to
answer."[36] He defines limiting questions as "an
utterance or inscription (sentence) which has the
grammatical structure of a question, but which does
not do the job of asking a straightforward question of
either a theoretical (What is the law of gravity?) or
practical (Should I vote for Smith?) sort."[37] They
are never literal questions, rather they express some
'inner' passion or action. Nielsen summarizes Coburn's
analysis thus:

Consider some responses to, 'What is

the ultimate significance of life?'
or 'What is the explanation of the
fact that there is a world at all?'
There are contexts in which questions are asked where there is no
straightforward answer or where no
literal answer is possible... Such
utterances arise out of despair or
anger or grief... or what occasions
them may be the engaging in a
'spiritual actitity', such as
'marvelling or worshipping or blas-
pheming.' Here we catch religious
discourse in one of its typical em-
ployments; and here religious
limiting questions find their
natural home.[38]

Coburn's next step is to classify such religious
limiting questions into three main categories, deriving from three kinds of problems: moral problems
(e.g., conflicts between duty and interest, conflicts
between moral outlooks, problem of handling guilt,
etc.); problems of morale ("those which arise out of
our inability to reconcile ourselves to the various
ills the flesh is heir to--sickness, failure...
death") and problems of meaning (i.e., concerning the
ultimate significance of things).[39]

Coburn then concludes that religious discourse is
discourse that is used to respond to such questions.
Theological language furnishes "logically complete
answers" to religious limiting questions. By
"logically complete answers," finally, he understands
"answers the acceptance of which by the person raising
the question is logically incompatible with his continuing to ask the question... "[40]

Nielsen, in response to Coburn, lauds his analysis
of the nondescriptive, noncognitive functions of religious discourse, since descriptive and cognitive functions lead necessarily to doctrinal complexities. But
he then accuses Coburn of missing the main point:

Coburn wishes to mark off a religious
use of language by way of an analysis
of religious limiting questions, which
will free our understanding of at
least some parts of religion from
these doctrinal perplexities. But like

23

the repressed they return to plague
him, for he is not able to specify
adequately what counts as "a religious limiting question.'[41]

There it is! The question that is critical in our investigation also: "What counts as a religious limiting
question?" David Tracy sets out specifically to address that question:

... I have come to believe that the
concept 'limit' can be used as a key
(but not exhaustive) category for describing certain signal characteristics peculiar to any language or experience with a properly religious
dimension. Whether that dimension be
explicit or implicit is not, in fact,
the central issue. My contention
will be that all significant explicitly religious language and experience
(the 'religions') and all significant
implicitly religious characteristics
of our common experience (the 'religious dimension') will bear at least the
'family resemblance' of articulating
or implying a limit-experience, a
limit-language, or a limit-dimension.
... Employed in our common discourse,
'religion' usually means a perspective
which expresses a dominating interest
in certain universal and elemental
features of human existence as those
features bear on the human desire for
liberation and authentic existence.
Such features can be analyzed as both
expressive of certain 'limits-to' our
ordinary experience (e.g., finitude,
contingency, or radical transcience)
and disclosive of certain fundamental
structures of our existence beyond
(or, alternatively, grounding to)
that ordinary experience (e.g., our
fundamental trust in the worthwhileness of existence, our basic belief
in order and value.[42]

The focal point then for Tracy is that even though "all
explicitly religious language and experience (the
religions) remain the most important expression of the

24

meaning of religion, still the claim can be made that
a certain basic horizon or dimension of our common
experience can justly be described as religious..."[43]

His objective therefore is to determine as nearly
as possible the religious dimension of our common
human experience and language through an analysis of
the limit-situations and/or limit questions of such
experiences. By "common human experience" Tracy intends not only our everyday human experiences, but
also our scientific, aesthetic, and moral experience.
An analysis of these (common human) experiences manifests both a final dimension to such experiences
(limit-to) and "witnesses to a dimension of ultimacy
(limit-of), a relation to an unconditional value,
order, certainty, and being beyond our making..."[44]
It is within these limit-situations that Tracy seeks
to find the 'religious dimension', and the appropriate
religious (metaphorical, symbolic, limit-) language.

Tracy then moves through a thorough and pains-
taking analysis of the limit questions in science and
in morality, and the limit situations in everyday
human experience, pointing up their religious dimension. I will not here repeat his analysis of the
religious dimension to scientific questions (e.g., Can
scientific answers work if the world is not intelligible? Can the world be intelligible if it does not
have an intelligent ground?, etc.), nor will I repeat
his analysis of the religious dimension to moral
limit-questions (e.g., Why ought I keep my promise?
Can we produce a moral argument for being moral?,
etc.), since these analyses would be too detailed for
our purposes and would perhaps be needlessly repetiti-
ous.[45] It will be sufficient for us here, in order to
see Tracy's methodology at work, to follow carefully
his analysis of the limit-situations in everyday life:

> ... limit-situations refer to two basic
> kinds of existential situation: either
> those 'boundary' situations of guilt,
> anxiety, sickness, and the recognition
> of death as one's own destiny, or those
> situations called 'ecstatic experiences'
> --intense joy, love, reassurance,
> creation. All genuine limit-situations
> refer to those experiences, both posi-
> tive and negative, wherein we both ex-
> perience our own human limits ('limit-to')

as our own as well as recognize, however, haltingly, some disclosure of
a 'limit-of' our experience...[46]

Whether, then, we analyze the negative kind of limit-
situations (which Karl Jaspers calls "boundary situations," i.e., anxiety, suffering, guilt, death)[47] or
the positive mode of limit-situations (Abraham
Maslow's "peak experiences" of love, joy, creativity,
trust, etc.),[48] we are in fact analyzing common human
experiences (not experiences of neurotics or in-
fatuated romantics):

> Beginning with Kierkegaard the classi-
> cal existential analyses of such ex-
> periences have provided a powerful way
> to clarify the human situation as in-
> trinsically a 'limit-situation': a
> situation wherein we find ourselves not
> the masters of our fate but radically
> contingent or limited ('boundary situa-
> tion'). At the same time we may also
> find ourselves as ecstatic, as gifted,
> even as 'graced'.[49]

What in fact this existential analysis manifests, to
paraphrase Tracy, is at the very least, "that the
final dimension or horizon of our own situation is
neither one of our own making nor one under our control."[50]

The final point in Tracy's analysis of limit-
situations and their religious dimension has to do
with the language we employ:

> .... at a certain point the language of
> conceptual analysis begins to falter.
> Instead, the human spirit begins to
> search for metaphor expressive of the
> experience (abyss, chasm, limit) and
> for narratives capable of expanding
> and structuring these metaphors (para-
> bles, myths, poems)... The language
> initially most appropriate for expres-
> sing that experience is symbolic as
> distinct from strictly conceptual lan-
> guage. Such language, as symbolic,
> involves a double intentionality which
> expresses both a literal meaning (e.g.,
> an actual physical abyss) and a non-

literal meaning which otherwise remains unsaid and unspoken (in this
case, the disclosure of another, a
final dimension, 'limit-to' our experience of the everyday and 'limit-
of' the rest of our existence).[51]

Concluding Tracy's analysis, then, we can assert
that limit-questions and limit-situations do disclose
the possibility of other dimensions to our lives beyond the ordinary day-to-day experiences. We have
spoken repeatedly of 'limit' whether limit-questions
or situations, as having a dual dimension, namely,
limiting or restricting, and grounding or disclosing.
We now have from Tracy's analysis terms specifically
designed to capture these two aspects of limit,
namely, "limit-to" our everyday, our moral, scientific,
and all other experiences, and "limit-of" such experiences (disclosive of possibility, grounding, etc.).
And so we conclude appropriately with Jaspers "...The
boundary situation thus plays its proper role of something immanent which already points to transcendence."[52]

Bringing to a close our reflections on this second
section regarding the distinction between limiting and
grounding, we can point with increasing precision to
the central theme emerging in our study, that is, that
'limit' is an essential category in analyzing the
multiple dimensions of human experience. We both emphasized the dual role that 'limit' plays, both 'limit-
to' (limiting, restricting) and 'limit-of' (disclosing,
grounding). We tied this back in with earlier conclusions, asserting thus that language is by nature
limited both in the sense of what it says (limit-to)
and what it does not say (limit-of).[53] Finally, the
overall experience of limit, whether of our everyday
experiences, or in the realms of science, morality, and
other areas should be characterized as religious (re-
presentative of a final dimension or horizon of meaning),
and the language appropriate to describe the experiences
as religious, or limit-language (both limiting and
grounding).[54] From this point on in this study, we will
adopt Tracy's distinction between 'limit-to' and 'limit-
of' as the ordinary way of distinguishing between the
two modes (dimensions) of limit, namely, limiting, restricting and constraining (limit-to) and disclosing,
grounding, liberating (limit-of). These two manifestations or dimensions of limit create conveniently the
context for our next question.

iii. <u>Limit and transcendence</u>. Perhaps the clearest
expression of the relationship between limit and transcendence was formulated by Wittgenstein. His contribution to this general question makes him a pivotal
figure in our discussion, since he stemmed the tide of
logical positivism (moving toward the elimination of
religious truths as significant) and opened up within
the context of language analysis itself the validity--
if not centrality--of religious (limit-) language.[55]

> Man has the urge to thrust against the
> limits of language. Think for instance
> about one's astonishment that anything
> exists. This astonishment cannot be
> expressed in the form of a question and
> there is no answer to it. Anything we
> can say must, a <u>priori</u>, be only non-
> sense. Nevertheless we thrust against
> the limits of language.... But the ten-
> dency, the thrust, <u>points to something</u>
> .... I can only say: I don't belittle
> this human tendency; I take my hat off
> to it.... For me the facts are unim-
> portant. But what men mean when they
> say that 'The world exists' lies close
> to my heart.[56]

Much has been written about Wittgenstein's notion of
the mystical, and his reflections on language, on the
inexpressible, and on limits all seem to lead in that
direction.[57] He himself writes again at the end of
his lecture on ethics:

> My whole tendency and I believe the
> tendency of all men who ever tried to
> write or talk on Ethics or Religion
> was to run against the <u>boundaries of</u>
> <u>language</u>. This running against the
> <u>walls of our cage</u> is perfectly, ab-
> solutely hopeless. Ethics, so far
> as it springs from the desire to say
> something about the meaning of life,
> the absolute good, the absolute valu-
> able, can be no science. What it says
> does not add to our knowledge in any
> sense. But it is a document of a
> tendency in the human mind which I
> personally cannot help respecting
> deeply and I would not for my life
> ridicule it.[58]

It would seem fairly clear, then, that Wittgenstein's own references move in the direction of the 'mystical'.[59] Concretely, his direct references to the mystical are contained primarily in the _Tractatus_, wherein he uses the word 'mystical' three times, to wit: "It is not how things are in the world that is mystical but _that_ it exists," and following that: "To view the world _sub specie aeterni_ is to view it as a whole--a limited whole. Feeling the world as a limited whole--it is this that is mystical." And, finally, "There are indeed, things that cannot be put into words. They _make themselves manifest_. They are what is mystical."[60]

For Wittgenstein, then, the mystical is linked with the inexpressible and, therefore, the transcendental. According to my colleague, Sister Elwyn McHale, the mystical is necessary for the unity and understanding of the _Tractatus_:

> According to Wittgenstein's notion of
> the world, the first part of the
> _Tractatus_ is inaccessible to man except
> in the attitude of _sub specie aeterni_.
> Without the world there is nothing to
> be shown to man in the mystical atti-
> tude; without the mystical the world
> as totality of facts is incomprehensi-
> ble. Only man in his transcendental
> attitude, viewing the world as a
> limited whole, can grasp the world as
> a totality of facts; and the essence
> of Wittgenstein's picture theory is
> that the world is the totality of
> facts, and only that.[61]

The key issue here then is that the limits of language manifest a dual character. They may have the appearance of barriers and boundaries (and indeed there is that profound human and religious experience of limit-to), but there is also the urge to push at these limits and these edges, a tendency toward that disclosure of a broader horizon or deeper ground (limit-of). It is this thrust, this urge, this tendency that opens up discussion about the transcendent. Approaching this question of transcendence and limit, we should take note of two preliminary points.

The first observation is advanced by Van Buren, and touches on the delicate maneuver of "pushing at

the edges" of language. He calls attention first to
an obvious point:

> .... There is no way in which we can
> lift ourselves out of our linguistic
> existence and survey the scene from
> some superior vantage point; we are
> unavoidably within the circle of lan-
> guage that we wish to understand.
> Consequently, we have difficulty
> thinking of the limits of that, be-
> yond which we cannot go and for which,
> by definition, we have no words....[62]

Van Buren continues to explore the meaning and import
of pushing at the limits of language, concluding that
perhaps what is needed is a clarification of the term
'limits',[63] since it presents "the picture of a line
that marks off one area within the limit from another
area beyond it... "[64] Using as an example the difference between a tennis court (outer lines, limits)
and a squash or racquetball court (there are no internal boundaries that "end" play; there is no "out,"
since everything is playable after the service), Van
Buren concludes: "So it is with our language. Language works up to the limits of our conventions, and
then it does not work at all."[65] Finally, suggesting
that the picture of language as a 'cage' instead of a
court might be contributing to the less than helpful
image of "inside-outside," Van Buren proposes a third
possibility, namely, the image of a platform on which
to stand as a model for seeing the role of language:

> .... on this platform we can move
> around, walk or dance or sleep, in-
> deed do all the things we do together
> with words. Far from imprisoning us,
> it gives us freedom. The planks of
> this platform are the rules for the
> use of words, and the planks are of
> various but determinate lengths.
> They stick out, as it were, only so
> far. If we wish to extend the plat-
> form, then we must build it out while
> standing on it. Language serves as
> the base on which we may stand in
> order to extend that base, and it is
> also (to mix our metaphors) the
> hammer and nails with which an exten-[68]
> sion to any plank must be secured..."

What is fairly obvious here is Van Buren's reliance
on the general Wittgensteinian notion of language
games, played by the rules, even changing the rules or
conventions from within. Once this image of language
game is secured, Van Buren's point is clear:

> .... We may speak better of the edges
> of language rather than of its limits.
> We can go so far out on the platform
> of language, but if we try to go fur-
> ther, we fall off into a misuse of
> words, into nonsensical jabbering, in-
> to the void where the rules give out.
> We can, on the other hand, if we are
> so inclined, walk right along the edge
> of language....[67]

Van Buren, exploring the notion of 'edge' of language
a bit further, concludes: "I wish to concentrate attention on the employment of words just short of this
total break with the rules for their use. I shall
speak of this employment as lying along 'the edges of
language'... "[68]

Van Buren's point, then, about the 'edges' of
language is well made. 'Limits' may very well suggest
a questionable notion of transcendence of "beyond."[69]
Although I think we have addressed that question adequately with Tracy's distinction between limit-to and
limit-of, nonetheless Van Buren's emphasis on the
discipline involved in the use of metaphor and story
(i.e., stretching language to its limits) is well
made, and we shall return to it in our discussion on
the theology of limit.

The second point to be noted regarding the urge
to thrust at the limits (edges) of language is articulated with precision by Crossan in his story about the
Lighthouse Keeper, a story that has two versions.
First, the centuries-old version of the classical mind:

> Once upon a time there were people who
> lived on rafts upon the sea. The rafts
> were constructed of materials from the
> land whence they had come. On this
> land was a lighthouse in which there
> lived a lighthouse keeper. No matter
> where the rafts were, and even if the
> people themselves had no idea where
> they actually were, the keeper always

knew their whereabouts. There was even
communication between people and keeper
so that in an absolute emergency they
could always be guided safely home to
land.[70]

For reasons that are imbedded in the history of the
last two centuries, this version of the story has become inadequate. The safe and somewhat secure relationship between the people and the keeper has been
challenged. Some, perhaps misreading what was actually happening, spoke about the "death of God";
others, perhaps more honestly, if not more accurately,
suggested that meaning had gone out of human existence.
Crossan in response proposes another version of the
Lighthouse Keeper:

There is no lighthouse keeper. There is
no lighthouse. There is no dry land.
There are only people living on rafts
made from their own imaginations. And
there is the sea.[71]

Stories create worlds. To challenge stories is to
challenge worlds. To tell new stories is to create
new worlds. Crossan's comment on his contemporary
version of the Lighthouse Keeper is thought-provoking:
"If there are only rafts and these rafts are really
language itself, what is the sea which is 'outside'
language because it is beyond the raft? Maybe there
is no sea either?"[72] These questions begin to get at
the same issues which bothered Van Buren in the images
of 'cage' and 'limits'. The "inside-outside" implica-
tion led him, it will be recalled, to choose the image
of 'edges' and the model of raft.[73] In fact, somewhat
later on in his Edges of Language, he addresses the
question of transcendence (God) more directly.[74]
Crossan continues here also to pinpoint the question
of transcendence in the context of limits:

.... If there is only language, then God
must be either inside language and in
that case, as I said above, an idol; or
he is outside language, and there is
nothing out there but silence. There is
only one possibility left, and that is
what we can experience in the movement
of the raft, in the breaks in the raft's
structure, and, above all, what can be
experienced at the edges of the raft

32

itself. For we cannot really talk of
the sea, we can only talk of the edges
of the raft and what happens there.
Our prayer will be, not 'Thank God for
edges,' but 'Thank edges for God.'[75]

To sum up, then, beginning with Wittgenstein's suggestion about the tendency to push at the limits of
language, adopting Tracy's notion of the limit-to and
limit-of language, incorporating Van Buren's image of
walking right along the edges of language, and,
finally, using Crossan's description of transcendence
and edges, we have been led systematically to a rather
well-determined perspective onto limit and transcendence. The very notion of limit-to (limiting, restricting, containing) has inherent in it the complementary notion of limit-of (grounding, disclosing,
liberating).[76] In other words, it is precisely--and
perhaps uniquely--in the experience of limit that
transcendence is realized. It is indeed there, at
the edges of language and borders of story, that one
experiences transcendence and ecstasy. As Rollo May
sums up in his The Courage to Create, ".... confronting limits for the human personality actually
turns out to be expansive. Limiting and expanding
thus go together."[77]

There remains one final point regarding the limit-
and-transcendence interface, that is, the genre of
literature within which limits, edges and borders are
most directly addressed, namely, the paradox-parable-
reversal dimension of story. It is for this reason
that Crossan devotes most of his study in The Dark
Interval to parable, that mode of story "deliberately
calculated to show the limitations of myth, to shatter
world so its relativity becomes apparent."[78] It is for
this reason also that Tracy follows his discussion of
religious and theological language as limit-language
with an investigation of the New Testament language,
especially of proverbs and parables.[79] We will explore story, myth, and parable directly in the next
section.

Some common threads should begin now to appear in
our discussion of language, limits, story, and finally
paradox and parable. Language creates world, so that
the limits of my language are the limits of my world.
But by language, of course, we understand story. And
so we return to our basic affirmation, story creates
world. Having said that, we are confronted inevitably

33

with limits, since our story is a story, and so necessarily limited. But we discussed a strong tendency within the human spirit to push against the boundaries and edges of language and story. That fact finally led to a fundamental theme in our entire study, namely, the experience of transcendence at that point precisely where limit seemed most absolute. We found that the language most appropriate for the creative task of challenging limits is the paradox-parable-reversal mode of narrative. Just as story has its mode of constructing and creating reality, namely, myth, so also story has its mode of 'deconstructing' and demythologizing, namely, parable. This dual function of story or narrative leads to our next discussion on theology of story and theology of limit.

iv. <u>Theology of story and theology of limit</u>. We have been weaving in and out of the relationship between story and limit for much of this chapter. We are ready now to address these two issues directly from the perspective of religious studies and theology. This will necessitate exploring each area individually, that is, first the theology of story and then the theology of limit, and then drawing some conclusions about the relationship between the two.

a. <u>Theology of story</u>. Much has been written on the theology of story over the last decade.[80] Although I do not propose to review that literature here, I do hope to select various themes which emerge from such a review, and which, woven together carefully, form a quite distinctive pattern.

The first theme I wish to highlight is the elusive character of story. We have spoken several times already of story as language-in-action, or narrative. Also, since we create worlds by the stories we tell, we found it essential to temper our rather impulsive urge to imagine a reality-world out there, objectively present, which <u>our</u> story <u>literally</u> represents. So we do not then intend by story the account of, or narrative about, an objective, absolute world out there. As Amos Wilder reminds us:

> Any human language represents a special kind of order superimposed upon existence. Generations live in it as a habitat in which they are born and die. Outside of it is nescience.... Perhaps one can say that nothing affects the significance of

> human existence more than the range
> and resource of our articulation,
> vocabulary, syntax and discourse.[81]

It is, therefore, to have come a long distance to have gone from the flippant, "It's just a story," to the stark realization that, "there's only story."

In our traditional discussions about story we have tended to lump together story and myth as virtually synonymous, distinguishing them--if at all--only on the basis of myth's being the overarching, comprehensive story which lays bare the structures of the world and makes clear to its adherents how to locate themselves in that world.[82] Although we still hear occationally the comment, "that's a myth," in the sense of opposition to "the real," by and large the work of Eliade, Levi-Strauss, and Ricoeur, have, to quote Ricoeur himself, begun to raise discourse to the "greatness of myth."[83] To move more responsibly, however, toward an understanding of story, it seems necessary to define more precisely the various kinds of story. Fortunately, at least to my mind, this task has been made noticeably easier by Crossan's suggestion that story is the general term for our narratives or accounts about ourselves in our world. Under the general term story, he distinguishes five modes or types of story, namely, myth, apologue, action, satire, and parable. He explains this classification:

> This gives us a full spectrum of story
> and the distinctions between its parts
> can best be explained by the relation-
> ship of each to world. It is these re-
> lationships, in other words, which es-
> tablish the different kinds of story,
> the different ways in story.... Myth
> establishes world. Apologue defends
> world. Action investigates world. Sa-
> tire attacks world. Parable subverts
> world....[84]

Of the various efforts to classify stories-myths, and we have mentioned especially Northrop Frye's classic division,[85] Crossan's classification of story into these five modes (myth, apologue, action, satire, and parable) seems more adaptable to the general pattern of stories. It not only sets a firm basis for distinguishing between story and myth (myth being one mode of story), but establishes also the other modes

35

of story, especially parable, so central both to the
Christian Story itself and to any theology of limit.

Our first point, then, about the elusive character
of story, might be summed up this way: Story is the
broadest category we have, since it is a narrative
about ourselves in our world. It is inaccurate simply
to identify story with myth (the account or narrative
about how world came to be, who we are in world, and
where we are going). Story, rather, ranges broadly
over apology, satire and ultimately parable. Parable
is that story which points up the limitation, relativity and inadequacy of myth. In this sense the
theology of limit is inherent in the theology of story,
as parable is somehow inherent in myth.[85] We shall return to the relationship between theology of story and
theology of limit later.

There is also a second theme running through the
literature on the theology of story, namely, the relationship between metaphor and analogy, or, in perhaps more traditional terms, literature and philosophy-
religion. Perhaps two questions might help focus the
issue more directly: How does theology move concretely
in the direction of metaphor and story, while at the
same time not abandoning the conceptual task so close
to its philosophical moorings? or What would theology
be like if it used the model of story (metaphor) rather
than the model of doctrine, dogma, and system?[86] Such
questions become especially pointed when one reflects
on the origin of Revelation (the story?) itself. Thus
Amos Wilder says:

> The narrative mode is uniquely important
> in Christianity... A Christian can confess
> his faith wherever he is, and without his
> Bible, just by telling a story or a series
> of stories... We see, then, that one of
> the earliest and most important rhetorical
> forms in the Church was the story. This
> is theoretically significant. The new
> movement of the Gospel was not to be
> identified with a new teaching or a new
> experience but with an action and there-
> fore a history.... [87]

We may see in these questions and comments a sound
basis on which theology of story should call to task
the strictly conceptual language of traditional religious and theological discourse. Brian Wicker addresses

this question directly:

> To anyone versed in history there should
> be nothing surprising about the rift be-
> tween the 'sophisticated' value-free
> language of the philosopher and the
> 'savage' metaphysical language of the
> poet and storyteller... The medieval
> philosophical synthesis of Aquinas and
> others, in which a highly developed
> theory of analogical language played a
> crucial part, was wrought at the expense
> of underplaying the importance of poetry
> and storytelling: that is to say, by
> undervaluing, or even misunderstanding
> the role of metaphorical language....[88]

Wicker goes on to decry the division between metaphor
and analogy in contemporary metaphysical language because of an out-of-hand rejection of the medieval
account of analogical predication by linguistic
philosophy. Wicker's fascinating essay (Story-Shaped
World) is an effort to reunite the two complementary
partners.[89]

A similar concern and corresponding effort is
supported by David Tracy:

> .... I have also come to insist that pre-
> cisely the concept of limit-language and
> the analysis of an originating symbolic
> religious dimension and an explicitly
> religious language provides an important
> new context for a reappropriation, not--
> as too many are tempted to suggest--an
> elimination of strictly conceptual lan-
> guage as well in religious and theologi-
> cal discourse... I have found myself
> turning more and more to a reinvestiga-
> tion of the conceptual language of both
> Thomas Aquinas himself and several repre-
> sentative and distinct modern Thomists,
> as providing examples of what I now call
> limit-concepts for religious and theolo-
> gical discourse....
> Finally, this same approach may pro-
> vide a new way to reappropriate Thomas'
> use of analogical language....[90]

What we see at work, then, both in Wicker's and in

Tracy's discussions of the complementarity of metaphor (narrative, story) and analogy (conceptual limit-language) is an effort to move concretely and resolutely in the direction of story (metaphor, narrative) and at the same time not to lose sight of the conceptual task which is so much a part of traditional theology and indeed of the philosophical mind itself.

Several comments occur to me regarding this distinction between metaphor and analogy. First, what seems to be under review here is what we might call, for the sake of understanding, first order and second order discourse. Thus story would be first order discourse, perhaps in the sense suggested earlier by Amos Wilder.[91] Metaphysical reflection and analogical elaboration on the other hand would be properly termed second order discourse (reflections on story). Although I can see merit in this kind of distinction, especially when it is articulated by Sallie Te Selle as parabolic theology,[92] there is at the same time an uneasy feeling that we might be back to the problem faced earlier in the question of a "real world," "out there," somehow waiting to be objectively described and narrated.[93] In other words, if, when we talk about story (metaphor, narrative) as first order discourse and analogy as second order discourse, we also assume-- ever so subtly--that such metaphysical reflections on story are somehow outside story, then we have fallen back into the trap of the story (master-story), or some similar absolutist position. That possibility, I suggest, is sufficient cause to counsel caution in the metaphor-analogy interface.

What is needed, perhaps, to guarantee adequate caution in the relationship between metaphor and analogy is simply to return to the distinction within story of its various modes, namely, myth, apologue, action, satire, and parable.[94] I think all the dimensions of human reflection are called into play in these five modes of story. We would generally see myth, that is, story by which world is constructed or established, as one pole, and parable, that is, story by which world is deconstructed or subverted, as the other pole in a bi-polar relationship.[95] Between myth and parable then we find a broad range of possibilities within story, namely, validation, justification, explanation, interpretation, and so forth. This clearly is all part of the theological task, and all of it is exercised within the context of story, indeed there is no other: it may be this story, or another story, but it is always story.

Given these kinds of cautionary reflections, I find the following methodology for the study of stories quite appropriate:

> Thus two of my most basic assumptions have been that in the study of stories, the matter of narrative rhetoric is crucial to a disciplined criticism, and that in the study of religious belief the matter of the adequacy of metaphysical foundations is equally crucial. But a third linking assumption has been that, in the nature of the case, religious belief is founded upon stories. Hence, bringing these seemingly quite distinct areas of study into some kind of mutual connection must involve relating the matter of narrative rhetoric and the matter of religious metaphysics. How is this to be accomplished? The burden of my answer has been this: that if we readily admit a rhetoric of fiction and a metaphysics of belief, it is equally important to recognize that there is a rhetoric of belief and a metaphysics of narrative.[96]

The task of bringing together in a mutually enriching way these seemingly quite distinct areas of study, namely, narrative rhetoric (story) and metaphysics of belief (religion, metaphysics), must be the central concern of the theology of story.

To elaborate further on this task, indeed challenge, I think, the theologian must take into account two crucial aspects of the story-dimension of religion (myth, satire, parable, etc.). It is not only, first, that a belief system (e.g., Christianity) is founded upon stories (incidentally, the stories most clearly attributable to Jesus were parables),[97] and that its vitality at any given time depends to a large extent upon the appropriate retelling of its story (stories), but, at the same time, and this is the critical interface between religion and literature, we need to know not only the rhetoric of the originating stories (myths, parables, proverbs, etc.), but we need to know the rhetoric of today's stories (or fiction), so that the re-telling will not only be faithful but dynamic and challenging.[98]

We have seen, then, the two major themes which
determine to a significant degree the meaning and function of the theology of story, namely, the nature of
story and its various modes, and, secondly, the relationship between story (metaphor) and analogy (metaphysics). As an appendage to these two central
themes, and a lead-in to the next section on the
theology of limit, a third theme relating to the
theology of story seems to require further attention,
and that is the relationship between the theology of
story and the notion of limit.[99] At the risk of overkill on the theme of story and limit, I think some
loose ends need to be tied together before proceeding
to the theology of limit. The major points to lift
out are three: First, the continuum, language-story-
limit, are, all three, essentially related, and we
have accepted the term 'story' for the generally narrative function of language. Secondly, story is by
nature limited, since it is our account about ourselves
and our world, thereby constructing (or deconstructing)
world in the process. The limit of story, finally, not
only serves to delimit or close (as limit-to), but also
to ground or disclose (as limit-of). And this leads us
directly from theology of story to theology of limit.

b. Theology of limit. It ought to be fairly clear at
this stage in our reflections that discussion on the
'theology of limit' both brings to conclusion the various issues considered earlier and also gives focus to
the following two parts of this essay, namely, the
limits of environment, and the limits of death. In
fact, the gradual progression from the general notion
of limit to the limits of language, followed by discussion of story and limit, and then to religious language
as limit-language, and, finally, to reflections on
theology of story--this gradual progression has led
logically to our central theme, the 'theology of limit'.

Perhaps, both as an opening statement about this
issue and as a point of departure for investigating its
several dimensions, we can begin with Crossan's suggestion regarding the function of any theology of limit.
"A theology of limit seeks above all to explore this
limitation, which is posed by the inevitability of life
within story, of existence in this story or that but
always in some story... "[100] The theology of limit,
then, follows from the theology of story as the specific
(or particular) follows from the general. And, as narrative about ourselves-in-our-world (constructing, ex-
plaining, justifying, questioning or deconstructing

40

world), story is necessarily particular (limited). It may indeed manifest universal elements, representing authentic possibilities of human existence (which also may explain the enduring character of world re- ligions),[101] but the very nature of cultural exchange --increasingly more widespread with the communications explosion--alerts one to other stories and experiences, and indeed even to the internal dynamism of one's own story. Awareness of these factors serves to remind one of the limits, boundaries, and edges of story-shaped world. It is the function of a theology of limit to foster this awareness, that is, to sensitize to the limit-questions, limit-situations, and limit-dimensions of human existence. In saying this, one almost feels the presence and power of the "Protestant principle," which brands even our best and noblest actions as in- acequate, and that precisely because they are _ours_. So it is with our _stories_.

If we have adequately announced the function of the theology of limit, then we might further describe its task as twofold: de-constructing or de-mythicizing and re-constructing or re-describing.[102] The first task of de-constructing follows logically from the impossibility of an objective, neutral world _out there_, which story describes more (sciences) or less (all other disci- plines) accurately. All that has been said here about language-story creating world, and the limits of lan- guage being the limits of world, undercuts the classic notion of "objective, neutral reality." Therefore, the theology of limit is entrusted with the unpopular task of de-construction (satiric and parabolic modes of story), that is, checking and challenging those claims of story (myth, apologue, action modes) to objective, absolute, and ultimately infallible standpoints.[103] At this point the theologians operating out of the model of 'limits' will have to be aware of two operations at work here, one external and the other internal. In other words, a theology of limit not only reflects back to every story (theory, system) its own relativity and limits, but also and at the same time must build self- conscious and self-critical reflection into its own methodology.[104] This description of the first task of the theology of limit is a somewhat more elaborate analysis of what we have been calling the limiting (limit-to) dimension of religious and theological lan- guage. In this sense, then, theology of limit tends to parallel the role of paradox-parable-reversal modes of story. Finally, although this function sometimes appears as negative and subversive, we call attention again to the very presence of disclosure (limit-of) in this limiting function: "Thank edges and limits for God."[105]

The second task entrusted to the theology of limit is to point up the other side of de-construction and de-mythicization or subversion, namely, re-construction and re-description. Within the very negation and limitation of status quo story (as myth), one sees presupposition and possibility (Phoenix phenomenon). The emphasis we have placed repeatedly on the limit-of dimension (disclosing, grounding) of religious and theological language requires that theology (of limit) participate in and indeed become the catalyst for re-description and re-presentation. The fact is that re-construction is woven into de-construction; parable does not just shatter or subvert reality, but in the very process creates a new reality.[106] Thus, for example, to assert that "Small is beautiful" (or, in a similar context, "Black is beautiful") is not only to effectively challenge and subvert a world where "big" is not only "beautiful," so to speak, but desirable and indeed essential to human success (everything is overkill, from cars to computers); it is simultaneously to construct an alternative world (or at least to open one up to that challenging possibility).[107]

It is at this point that theology of limit and theology of story participate in a common methodology, that is, a method of telling (re-constructing, re-describing, re-presenting) the traditional stories in the language and idiom appropriate to a new and different time and place. Such a methodology requires two special skills for its effective implementation, namely, those of the (linguist and) literary critic, on the one hand (knowledge of the rhetoric of narrative), and those of the Biblical specialist and theologian (knowledge of the religious stories) on the other. Brian Wicker gives some direction to this seemingly Herculean task:

> But a belief system such as Christianity is not only founded upon stories; its articulation at any particular moment of a society's history, the flesh and blood of its living reality (or indeed, the overt lack of it) largely depends upon that society's ability to tell itself the appropriate kinds of story. We have therefore to consider not

only the rhetoric of the founding narratives, we must also consider the
rhetoric of today's fictions.[108]

What is demanded, then, in telling the "appropriate
kind of story" (re-construction, re-description, re-
presentation) is first a sense of the rhetoric of narrative, that is, the rhetoric not only of the "founding
narratives" or originating stories (myth, parable,
proverb, etc.), but also of current fiction (novel,
parable, poetry, short story, satire). A second re-
quirement for our theologian (of story and limit) is
that she be aware of the metaphysics of religious belief. In other words, that she be attuned to the assumptions of the community contained in their stories.
Concretely, for example, to re-present the religious
(metaphysical) presuppositions in the telling of the
story of <u>evil</u> (original sin or primordial catastrophe)
will require more than average theological dexterity.[109]

This function of the theology of limit (in the
overall scheme of the theology of story) is best sum-
marized under our technical description of the
grounding, disclosing (limit-of) dimension of religious
and theological language, that is, "when the human
spirit begins to search for metaphors expressive of the
experience (abyss, chasm, limit) and for narratives
capable of expanding and structuring these metaphors
(parables, myths, poems)."[110]

c. <u>Relationship between theology of limit and theology
of story</u>. Much is already evident about the relation
between these two modes of theology from the discussion
just concluded. First of all, the theology of limit is
a significant and indispensable dimension of the theology of story. Theology of limit first accentuates the
limit-to language and story, that is, their limitation
and relativity (or relationality), and in this sense
functions much like the parabolic (paradox-reversal)
mode of story. Theology of limit also suggests the
possibilities disclosed in the experience of limitation
and relativity (limit-of), possibilities for re-construction, re-presentation, indeed re-creation (new
story creates new world). And the process goes on: as
world (created by story which is myth) is subverted by
story which is parable (limit-to), so world is re-
created by story which is myth (limit-of).... These
limit-dimensions of human experience are what we rightly
call religious experiences:

43

> .... extraordinary moment(s) of aware-
> ness or transformation of awareness
> (limit-to) which subsequently alter(s)
> one's mode of self-conscious being-in-
> the-world (limit-of). That is, it (they)
> alter(s) one's perception of oneself as
> self and person, and consequently one's
> manner of living, of relating to one's
> surroundings....[111]

The language most appropriate to these experiences, of
course, is authentically religious language, the limit-
language of metaphor (story) and analogy.

We have noted, finally, that it is precisely at
those moments of limit-to our worlds, experiences, and
projects (whether boundaries or ecstasies) that new
horizons, new possibilities, new worlds are disclosed
(limit-of our world). We have characterized this
phenomenon as transcendence at the limits, boundaries,
and edges. What should be clear, then, is that we
have been gradually shifting emphasis away from the
"God of the gaps" and to the gaps, cracks, and chinks
where transcendence (God) is experienced. This is expressive both of the limit of theology and the theology
of limit.[112]

3. CONCLUSION: LIMITS OF LANGUAGE AS CONTEXT

There are two issues I wish to address in concluding the first part of this essay. I want first to
draw together some of the common threads running
through our reflections so far; secondly, I want to suggest the manner in which the following two parts of this
essay, namely, limits of environment and limits of
death, are derived from and related to the limits of
language.

The common threads characterizing our reflection
up to this point can probably be summed up in several
key words and phrases: language, limits, limit-language, story, theology of story, and theology of limit.
There is also a kind of logical tying together of these
concepts in the notion of theology of limit. Theology
of limit is best understood as an essential function of
the theology of story, accentuating, that is, the para-
bolic-paradoxical-reveral dimension of story. Theology
of story, on the other hand, captures the reality of
story as the central human--and therefore religious--
experience. Story in turn, as language-in-action,

44

manifests the limits within which we all live. Limit,
finally, can be restricting or liberating; limiting or
grounding; constraining or disclosing; and we are back
to the theology of limit, that is, limit-to and limit-
of dimension of human and thence religious experience.

The second issue I want to address is the relationship between language and the experience of limit,
our first area of investigation, and the next two
areas, namely, environment and the experience of limit
and death and the experience of limit. We will be exploring this relationship primarily in terms of two
relatively firm points of contact: first, the revealing similarity among the three contexts or experiences of limit: language (story is all there is); environment (nature shall have the last word); and death
(I am and I will die[113]); secondly, the striking realization that in all three discussions of limit-experiences, language, environment, and death, metaphor and
story are the primary modes of discourse. We have already argued this point in discussing the language
adequate to and appropriate for the limit-questions
and limit-situations of human experience in general.
Let the following quotes be a preliminary verification
of the need for metaphor and story (myth, poetry, etc.)
in the limit-experience of environment and the limit-
situation of death:

> One of the most exciting and vital kinds
> of poetry being written in this country
> is nature poetry...
> The nature poets of our time charac-
> teristically approach their subject with
> an openness of spirit and imagination,
> allowing the meaning and the movement of
> the poem to suggest themselves out of the
> facts. Their art has an implicit and es-
> sential humility, a reluctance to impose
> on things as they are, a willingness to
> relate to the world as student and ser-
> vant, a wish to be included in the
> natural order rather than to conquer
> nature, a wish to discover the natural
> form, rather than to create new forms
> that would be exclusively human. To
> create is to involve oneself as fully,
> as consciously and imaginatively, as
> possible in the Creation, to be immersed
> in the world....[114]

It seems that death and poetry belong together in at least three ways. To create, the poet must be ready for death in order to allow the poem to come forth. To receive the poem, one must surrender to death too, for the poem reveals Being in a new and original way. And finally, the poem itself affirms death in saying the whole; the poem sings existence as a whole....[115]

To end the first part of this essay and introduce the second and third parts, two poems, the first by Ezra Pound, the second by Rainer Maria Rilke, will speak to us in stories ways of man and environment and man and death:

The ant's a centaur in his dragon world.
Pull down thy vanity, it is not man
made courage, or made order, or made grace,
Pull down thy vanity, I say pull down.
Learn of the green world what can by thy
place.[116]

But because being here is much, and because
all this
that's here, so fleetingly, seems to require us and strangely
concerns us. Us the most fleeting of all.
Just once,
everything, only for once. Once and no
more. And we, too,
once. And never again. But this
having been once, though only once,
having been once on earth--can it ever be
cancelled?[117]

CHAPTER II NOTES

1. The Collected Poems of Wallace Stevens (New York: Alfred A. Knopf, 1955), p. 300.

2. The Latin phrase carries more humor, "De omni re scibili et de quibusdam aliis."

3. Particularly helpful to me in this study were: William Barrett, The Illusion of Technique (Garden City, NY: Anchor Press/Doubleday, 1978); Edward Cell, Language, Existence, and God (Nashville: Abingdon, 1971); K. T. Fann, Wittgenstein's Conception of Philosophy (Berkeley: University of California Press, 1969); A. Janik and S. Toulmin, Wittgenstein's Vienna (New York: Simon & Schuster, 1972).

4. See, for example, Brian Davies, "Wittgenstein on God," Philosophy, 55: 1980, pp. 105-108; N. H. G. Robinson, "After Wittgenstein," Religious Studies, 12: 1976, pp. 493-507; Cyril Barrett (Ed.), Wittgenstein: Lectures & Conversations on Aesthetics, Psychology & Religious Belief (Berkeley: University of California Press, 1972).

5. George Sefler, Language and the World (Atlantic Highlands: Humanities Press, 1974), p. 195.

6. See, for example, George Sefler, Language and the World. Also, Thomas Dean, Post-Theistic Thinking (Philadelphia: Temple U. Press, 1975), pp. 171-195, and Thomas A. Fay, "Heidegger & Wittgenstein on the Question of Ordinary Language," Philosophy Today, 23: 1979, pp. 154-159.

7. Tractatus Logico-Philosophicus (Translated by D. F. Pears, and B. F. McGuiness, London: Routledge & Kegal Paul, 1961), 5.6.

8. Tractatus, 5.61, 5.62. Max Black (Companion to the 'Tractatus') suggests that in this passage we should read bedeuten as 'are': "The passage would then read: 'The limits of my world are the logical possibilities which the language I use in talking about it gives to me." (T. Martland, "On 'The Limits of Language Mean the Limits of My World'," Review of Metaphysics, 29: 1975, pp. 19-26.

9. Holderlin and the Essence of Poetry (quoted in
   George Sefler, Language and the World, op. cit.,
   p. 188).

10. Sefler, op. cit., p. 189.

11. See T. Martland, art. cit., p. 19:
    If the limits of the language which I use does
    mean the limits of the world which I know, that
    language must impose itself upon this world.
    If the language which I use imposes itself up-
    on my world this imposition must contribute to,
    or participate in, this world which I know be-
    cause of it. That is, it cannot merely point
    to it, but must actually bring it about. (p.
    19)

12. See above, p. 9.

13. Philosophical Investigations (Oxford: Blackwell,
    1953), 4, 121.

14. The Edges of Language, p. 45.

15. Ibid., p. 57.

16. See Walker Percy, Message in a Bottle (New York:
    Farrar, Strauss & Giroux, 1975), p. 7, 150.

17. Later on in this essay we will distinguish more
    clearly between 'story' and 'myth'.

18. See Northrop Frye, Anatomy of Criticism (Prince-
    ton, N.J.: Princeton University Press, 1957),
    pp. 158-239.

19. See John D. Crossan, The Dark Interval, p. 9.

20. Northrop Frye, op. cit. See also Frank Mc
    Connell, Story-telling and Myth-making (New York:
    Oxford U. Press, 1979), pp. 1-20. Later in this
    essay we will investigate and incorporate into
    this study the modes of story discussed by John
    D. Crossan, op. cit., pp. 47-62.

21. One might call to mind here the criminal connota-
    tions of "subversive" and "subversive elements."
    They are indeed subversive who challenge the ex-
    isting myth (story) thru satire, paradox, and
    parable.

22. See above, notes 7, 8, for the original quote from Wittgenstein.

23. The Dark Interval, p. 14.

24. The Edges of Language, p. 45.

25. David Tracy, "Religious Language as Limit-Language," Theology Digest, 22: 1974, pp. 291-307. See, also, Blessed Rage for Order: The New Pluralism in Theology (New York: Seabury, 1975), chapters 4 and 5.

26. David Tracy, "Religious Language as Limit-Language," p. 291.

27. Paul Van Buren, The Edges of Language, p. 83.

28. Ibid.

29. See A. Janik and S. Toulmin, Wittgenstein's Vienna (New York: Simon & Schuster, 1972), pp. 232-235.

30. See D. Tracy, Blessed Rage for Order, p. 111 (n. 11).

31. David Tracy, "Religious Language as Limit-Language," p. 291.

32. Ibid., p. 292.

33. See Stephen Toulmin, An Examination of the Place of Reason in Ethics (Cambridge: Cambridge U. Press, 1950, pp. 204ff.

34. Kai Nielsen, "Religion, Science and Limiting Questions," Sciences Religieux, 8: 1979, pp. 259-265.

35. Robert C. Coburn, "A Neglected Use of Theological Language," Mind, 72: 1963, pp. 368-385.

36. Ibid., 371.

37. Ibid.

38. Nielsen, art. cit., p. 262.

39. Coburn, art. cit., pp. 373f.

40. Ibid., p. 375.

41. Nielsen, art. cit., p. 264.

42. David Tracy, Blessed Rage for Order, p. 93.

43. Ibid.

44. Langdon Gilkey, Religion and the Scientific Future (New York: Harper and Row, 1970), p. 62.

45. See Tracy, op. cit., pp. 94-104; also Langdon Gilkey, op. cit., pp. 34-64.

46. David Tracy, "Religious Language as Limit-Language," p. 292.

47. Karl Jaspers, Philosophy (Translated by E. B. Ashton, Chicago: University of Chicago Press, 1970):
    Situations like the following: that I am always in situations; that I cannot live without struggling and suffering; that I cannot avoid guilt; that I must die--these are what I call boundary situations. They never change, except in appearance..." (vol. 2, p. 178).
    See also the pointed commentary by Wesley Kort, Narrative Elements and Religious Meaning (Philadelphia: Fortress Press, 1975), pp. 36-37.

48. Abraham Maslow, Toward a Psychology of Being (Princeton, NJ: D. Van Nostrand, 1968):
    I would like you to think of the most wonderful experience or experiences of your life; happiest moments, ecstatic moments, moments of rapture, perhaps from being in love, or from listening to music or suddenly 'being hit' by a book or painting, or from some great creative moment.... (p. 71).

49. David Tracy, art. cit., p. 294.

50. Ibid.

51. Ibid., p. 295.

52. Karl Jaspers, op. cit., p. 179.

53. The relationship between the 'language of silence' and religious language opens up a fertile area for reflection. Wittgenstein's comments on his Tractatus are instructive: "My work consists of two parts: the one presented here plus all that I have not written. And it is precisely this second part that is the important one." (Cited in K. T. Fann. Wittgenstein's Conception of Philosophy, p. 1). Also, Wesley Kort makes some thought-provoking comments on the role of silence in religious language (Narrative Elements and Religious Experience, pp. 10-11.

54. David Tracy discusses the appropriateness of using the term 'religious' for limit-language, especially in view of such alternative suggestions as Ramsey's 'odd' language (Blessed Rage for Order, pp. 131-133).

55. See A. Janik and S. Toulmin, Wittgenstein's Vienna, pp. 219-238. Also William Barrett, The Illusion of Technique, pp. 51-57.

56. "Wittgenstein's Lecture on Ethics," Philosophical Review 74:1965, pp. 13-16.

57. I have been fortunate enough to have at hand the doctoral dissertation of my colleague, S. Elwyn McHale, The Notion of the Mystical in Wittgenstein's Tractatus (Washington, D.C.: The Catholic University of America, 1977).

58. "Wittgenstein's Lecture on Ethics," pp. 11-12.

59. See C. H. Cox and J. Cox, "The Mystical Experience: With an Emphasis on Wittgenstein and Zen," Religious Studies, 12: 1976, pp. 483-491. Also William Barrett, The Illusion of Technique, pp. 51ff.

60. Tractatus, 6.44, 6.45, 6.52.

62. Paul Van Buren, The Edges of Language, p. 83.

63. We have already discussed the different ways in which the term 'limit' is used by Van Buren, Tracy, and Ricoeur (see above, pp. 21).

64. Paul Van Buren, op. cit., p. 82.

65. Ibid.

66. Ibid.

67. Ibid., p. 83. I think Tracy's refinement of the notion of limit as both 'limit-to' and 'limit-of' answers this concern of Van Buren. One is reminded in this regard of T. S. Eliot's description: "Words strain/crack and sometimes break, under the burden." (Burnt Norton).

68. Ibid., p. 84. See, also, an interesting discussion of metaphor and limit by Ann Clark, "Metaphor and Literal Language," Thought, 52: 1977, pp. 366-380, especially pp. 372ff.

69. Paul Van Buren, op. cit., pp. 146f.

70. John D. Crossan, The Dark Interval, p. 41. This brings to mind also Paul Van Buren's model of 'rafts' and 'edges'.

71. Ibid., p. 44.

72. Ibid.

73. See, above, p. 20.

74. Van Buren addresses the problem thus:
    ... The mistake is to think that the word 'God' either falls well within the edges of language, where religious claims about God would be meaningful but would appear to be false, or else outside language altogether. It seems evident to me now that the word had never had much life in either of these foreign soils. Planted in its own ground, however, right on, and marking, the boundary of language, the word can be as alive and flourishing today as in the past ... Saying 'God' is an acknowledgement that one has come to the end of language (op. cit., p. 144).

75. Crossan, op. cit., pp. 44f. Although there is some similarity to Van Buren's comments above (n. 74), Crossan has some particular nuances that deserve emphasis.

76. The notion of complementarity between limit-to
    and limit-of language suggests an example of
    the "yin/yang" complementary opposition of
    Taoism.

77. Rollo May, The Courage to Create, p. 115.

78. Crossan, op. cit., p. 60.

79. Tracy, op. cit., pp. 119ff.

80. Besides Crossan's The Dark Interval: Toward a
    Theology of Story, especially helpful to me were:
    Wesley A. Kort, Narrative Elements and Religious
    Meaning (Philadelphia: Fortress Press, 1975);
    Sallie Te Selle, Speaking in Parables (Phila-
    delphia: Fortress Press, 1975); Brian Wicker,
    Story-Shaped World (Notre Dame, IN: University of
    Notre Dame Press, 1975); James B. Wiggins (ed.),
    Religion as Story (New York: Harper & Row, 1975).

81. Amos N. Wilder, The Language of the Gospel: Early
    Christian Rhetoric (New York: Harper & Row, 1964),
    pp. 13-14.

82. This is a feeble attempt to paraphrase Eliade's
    description of myth. See Mircea Eliade, "Method-
    ological Remarks on the Study of Religious
    Symbolism," in The History of Religions (ed.
    Mircea Eliade and Joseph Kitagawa, Chicago:
    University of Chicago Press, 1959), pp. 86-107.

83. See Paul Ricoeur, The Symbolism of Evil (New York:
    Harper & Row, 1967), p. 236.

84. Crossan, The Dark Interval, p. 59. He is following
    Sheldon Sacks' Fiction and the Shape of Belief.

85. See above, in our discussion about language and
    story.

86. See Sallie Te Selle, op. cit., pp. 138ff.

87. Amos Wilder, The Language of the Gospel, p. 76.

88. Brian Wicker, Story-Shaped World, pp. 7f.

89. Ibid., p. 214.

90. Tracy, "Religious Language as Limit-Language," pp. 302-304. See, also, Tracy's recent work, The Analogical Imagination (New York: Crossroad, 1981).

91. The Language of the Gospel, p. 76.

92. Sallie Te Selle, op. cit., pp. 164ff.

93. See above, Part I.

94. See above, p. 43.

95. Crossan, op. cit., p. 52.

96. Brian Wicker, op. cit., p. 214.

97. For a sample of recent work done on the Parables, see John Dominic Crossan, In Parables (New York: Harper & Row, 1973); also, Crossan's Dark Interval (op. cit.), and Norman Perrin, Jesus and the Language of the Kingdom (Philadelphia: Fortress Press, 1976).

98. This kind of function, it seems, would give pretty clear definition to the field of religion and literature. See Sallie Te Selle, "Story: Rising and Chameleon Genre," Review of Books in Religion, 5: 1976, p. 1f.

99. Obviously, this is an appendage in format only, since the question of story and limit have been central in this study.

100. John D. Crossan, The Dark Interval, p. 14.

101. See Huston Smith, Forgotten Truth: The Primordial Tradition (New York: Harper and Row, 1976), pp. ixf. Smith describes what has been called the 'perennial philosophy' (philosophia perennis) as 'primordial tradition', or simply, 'tradition'.

102. I am not using the term, 'de-constructing', in the technical sense in which it has come to be used by Jacques Derrida and other poststructuralist philosophers.

103. On the proper understanding of 'standpoint', see Michael Novak, Ascent of the Mountain, Flight of the Dove, p. 53.

104. See Crossan, op. cit., p. 47.

105. See above, p. 39.

106. This is more of a Phoenix-like phenomenon. The ashes are not just ashes, since the alternative story is already rising in the shattering of the old.

107. The same kind of approach might be used to describe the "Black is Beautiful" story. To say that is to both deconstruct the myth of "black is ugly, dirty, sinister, etc.," and at the same time to construct a new myth of the beauty, value, worthwhileness, power, soul, etc. of "black."

108. Brian Wicker, Story-Shaped World, p. 214.

109. See David Tracy, Blessed Rage for Order, pp. 212 ff.

110. Tracy, "Religious Language as Limit-Language," p. 295.

111. Sallie B. King, "Concepts, Anti-Concepts and Religious Experience," Religious Studies, 14: 1978, 445-458. See p. 446. The parentheses are mine.

112. What I intend here by the 'limits of theology' is that in a sense theology, too, must recognize that, even though it is describing and representing limit-questions and limit-situations of human experience (depth-dimensions, as it were), this, too, is story. As Dominic Crossan notes in a slightly different context: "... (we) have taken the necessity of story as our master-story." Op. cit., p. 47.

113. See John Dunne, The Reasons of the Heart (New York: Macmillan, 1978), pp. 148-194.

114. Wendell Berry, "A Secular Pilgrimage," in Western Man and Environmental Ethics (Ed. by Jan Barbour, Menlo Park, California: Addison-Wesley, 1973), pp. 132f.

115. Linda Leonard, "The Belonging-together of Poetry
      and Death," Philosophy Today, 19: 1975, pp. 137-
      145. See p. 144.

116. The Cantos of Ezra Pound (New York: New Direc-
      tions, 1972), p. 521.

117. R. M. Rilke, Selected Works: II. Poetry (New
      York: New Directions, 1967), p. 244.

CHAPTER III

ENVIRONMENT AND THE EXPERIENCE OF LIMIT

> Our eyes do not divide us from the world,
> but unite us with it ... Let us abandon
> the simplicity of separation and give
> unity its due. Let us abandon the self-
> mutilation which has been our way and
> give expression to the potential harmony
> of man-nature ... Man is that uniquely
> conscious creature who can perceive and
> express. He must become the <u>steward of</u>
> <u>the biosphere</u>. To do this he must <u>design</u>
> <u>with</u> <u>nature</u>.

"Steward of the biosphere" and "design with
nature" are rich images which portray quite accurately
the general thrust of these reflections on environment
and the experience of limit. Before tackling this
issue, however, I think two introductory comments may
be helpful; first, some comments regarding the relationship between language as a context of limit (limits
of language) and environment (nature) also as a context
of limit; second, further comments about the implications of the limits of environment for a theology of
limit.[2]

First, comparing the two contexts of limits within which inevitably human existence is lived, that is,
language and environment, we note that they are both
similar and different. As contexts of limits, language
and environment are similar because of their comprehensive and all-encompassing character. They both cir-
cumscribe human existence. There is both the awareness of nature (environment) surrounding, pervading,
encompassing and threatening humanity, and simultaneously humanity feeling, speaking, singing, and writing
about that experience. Robinson Jeffers in his <u>The</u>
<u>Beauty of Things</u> captures the interplay well:

> To <u>feel</u> and <u>speak</u> the astonishing beauty of
>   things--earth, stone and water,
> Beast, man and woman, sun moon and stars--
> The blood-shot beauty of human nature, its
>   thoughts, frenzies and passions,
> And unhuman nature its towering reality--
> For man's half dream; man, you might say, is

<pre>
             nature dreaming, but rock
        And water and sky are constant--to feel
        Greatly, and understand greatly, and ex-
             press greatly, the natural
        Beauty, is the sole business of poetry.[3]
</pre>

In a virtual embrace person and environment are locked
together, human immersed in natural, almost denying,
as it were, the distinction between man[4] and nature.
Yet, it is (the) person who is not only experiencing,
but describing the experience. That we can "_feel_ the
beauty of things" already presupposes language; that
we can "_speak_ the beauty of things" tests the creative
possibility (pushing at the limits) of language, that
is poetry.[5] Our analysis, then, tends to separate
language and environment for the sake of understanding,
but one does feel nonetheless a tinge of guilt for
violating a rather intimate union. Returning to
Wittgenstein's classic statement, "language creates
world; the limits of my language are the limits of my
world,"[6] we begin perhaps to understand even more fully
the impact of that concept.

   If the similarity between language and environment, as comprehensive contexts for the experience of
limit, is fairly obvious, equally striking is the difference.[7] The difference in a word is that there is
no vantage point outside of language to consider language, whereas humans can stand apart (in our consciousness) from the environment. To repeat some of
the conclusions from the first part of this essay, we
emphasized the inability of humans to get outside of
language to talk about language. "To determine what
counts as language uses rules already found in some
language as 'counting'."[8] To put it another way,
perhaps:

             What can be thought can be put into words
             and what cannot be put into words cannot
             be thought... There are no unutterable
             thoughts; all thoughts are linguistic in
             character, for indeed the way of speaking
             is the way of thinking.[9]

Even to talk about environment/nature, then, is to be
in story (harmony-naturalism; domination; stewardship;
conservation; earthkeeping, etc.). Even though the
world (nature/planet) may be _there_ (objectively and
concretely), it always _in fact_ is there subjectively,

that is, present to me (and us), and what it is besides this doesn't matter. "How we speak about the world reveals the world about which we are speaking."[10] Finally, then, since thinking depends upon language we cannot conceive of that for which we have no words.

This identification between language and experience differentiates language from environment as contexts of human limitation. We can, in fact, "stand outside of" (ex-sistere) our natural environment.[11] In other words, we can stand apart from nature/environment (at least in our consciousness); we can reflect on our world in the context of the story which brought it into being (myth, explanation, justification, criticism, reversal are all modes such reflection may take).[12] Our environment, to repeat, is our creation (story); we can change that story (de-construction/re-construction) from within precisely because it is story (myth) and therefore necessarily and inevitably limited.

To conclude, language and environment are similar in that they both, as contexts for the human experience of limit, manifest similar characteristics of comprehensiveness and circumscription. At the same time they are significantly different, since the nature of that circumscription and comprehensiveness in the case of environment is not absolute and total. Humans can in fact reflect on their environment (that is, the story about nature/planet) as the context for human-being-in-the-world. The same is not true of language; immersion in language is absolute and total: we cannot even think without words. For this reason we have insisted upon the fact that language is the paradigmatic experience of limit. Environment and death as experiences of limit are perhaps best described as "signs and reminders of this more fundamental limit (of language)."[13]

This discussion of limit leads into the second introductory comment regarding the application of the theology of limit to the issue of environmental limits. In an earlier discussion of methodology we determined as the primay objective of a theology of limit sensitization to, and awareness of the limit-situations and limit-questions of human experience (what we have also described as the inevitable limits of living within story). This objective of a theology of limit, it was also determined, is further specified by two dimensions of limit and their related functions: 1) Limit-to-experience, that is, the parabolic-reversal function of

59

de-construction and de-mythicization, and 2) <u>Limit-of-experience</u>, namely, the mythical-integral function of representation and reconstruction. It is the application of these functions of the theology of limit to the limit-situations of man* and environment that dictates the format for the second part of this essay, a format consisting of three chapters: 1) Limit-to-environment; 2) Limit-of-environment; 3) Religious (Limit-) language and ecology.

1. Limit-to Enviroment

> The ant's a centaur in his dragon world.
> Pull down thy vanity, it is not man
> made courage, or made order, or made grace,
> > Pull down thy vanity, I say pull down.
> Learn of the green world what can be thy
> > place
> In scaled invention or true artistry,
> Pull down thy vanity...[14]

These few lines of Ezra Pound's <u>Canto LXXXVI</u> might properly serve as the epigraph for our study of limit-to-environment. The issue here specifically is about the concrete experience of limitation, restriction and constraint. In the area of man and environment the task of de-mythicization and de-construction has been underway for some time. This effort in fact already possesses some characteristics of a new myth. Our challenge here, then, is somewhat delicate. On the one hand, we want to reverse the story about man* and environment, so that contemporary man* can see it clearly <u>as</u> story, and therefore as inherently relative; on the other hand, we don't want to intimate that there is lurking someplace in the wings an absolute and final story about man*-in-nature, which needs only to be substituted for the current myth.

What we shall be doing, then, is telling a story about planet earth which relies rather heavily on the current accounts from the science of ecology. Further, by lacing this account with a healthy dose of metaphor and poetry, we hope to <u>keep</u> ourselves alerted to the reality of story. Our narrative will be characterized by four generally shared impressions about planet earth at the present time: i) The planet as a closed system; ii) The complexity of the system; iii) Humankind as part of the ecosystem; and iv) The delicate balance within the system. Much has been written, at least in

the last decade, about the science of ecology.[15] It
is both beyond my expertise and too extensive even to
summarize here. I will merely allude in passing to
the basic significance of these four generalizations
about our eco-story.

i. <u>Planet earth is a closed system</u>. There are currently a number of assumptions about our planet-and-
us-in-it which undergird this statement. Perhaps it
would be helpful here to lift out two of these assumptions for closer examination, namely, the planet as a
'system' and the notion of a 'closed' system.

First, to speak of planet earth as a system signals a major shift in our contemporary science from an
atomistic, individualistic paradigm of reality to a
holistic and systems approach. The general function
operative here is known as systems analysis. As Ervin
Laszlo points out:

> ... To have an adequate grasp of reality
> we must look at things as systems, with
> properties and structures of their own.
> Systems of various kinds can then be
> compared, their relationships within
> still larger systems defined, and a
> general context established. If we are
> to understand what we are, and what we
> are faced with in the social and the
> natural world evolving a general theory
> of systems is imperative.[16]

Further, to speak of planet earth as a system is to
incorporate the broadest possible range of relationships, short of interplanetary systems, under that
model. In this connection Laszlo suggests a very
helpful modification:

> A systems science can look at a cell or
> an atom as a system, or it can look at
> the organ, the organism, the family, the
> community, the nation, the economy, and
> ecology as systems, and it <u>can view even
> the biosphere as such</u>. A system in one
> perspective is a subsystem in another.[17]

To repeat, speaking of planet earth as a system,
we are adopting the broadest systematic model, namely,
the biosphere, that is, the total biotic or living
community and its nonliving environment. This

scientific image challenges the imagination to envision
all of the interrelationships among the myriad elements
(over a million species of living things) in this system. Perhaps something like this is behind Wallace
Stevens' poetic reflections in <u>Esthetique du Mal</u>:

> To love sensibility, to see what one sees,
> As if sight had not its own miraculous
>   thrift,
> To hear only what one hears, one meaning
>   alone,
> As if the paradise of meaning ceased
> To be paradise, it is this to be
>   destitute.[18]

The shorthand term for this complex system of
living groups in the non-living environment in which
they function is <u>eco-system</u>. Information about the
ecosystem and the study of the eco-system is what we
have come to call the science of ecology, that is,
the interaction between living organisms and their
environment.

The second assumption about our earth as a system
is that it is a <u>closed</u> or <u>finite</u> system. There is an
interesting linguistic turn involved here. We have
accentuated throughout this essay that limit is an
integral part of story. Now in this story about ecosystem we have the story itself (already implying
'limit') emphasizing the reality of limits. In any
event, to say that our eco-system is finite is to intimate at least two possible scenarios: first, the
common-sense fact that living organisms must move
within definite limits, since they cannot use more
energy, more food, and more nutrients than are available. The second meaning appears more abstract and
theoretical, based as it is on the laws of thermodynamics and the threat of so-called "heat death."
Simply put, the second law of thermodynamics states
that energy is finite, that is, that the sun is a
limited source. But every change (synthetic) requires
a certain output of energy (given off as heat).
Clearly, there will come a time--or a point in time--
when there simply will be no more energy, and the
whole process, one might say, will come to a screeching
halt.[19] Whether one adopts the common-sense approach
(and takes seriously the conservation of our resources), or whether we allow the "heat-death" image
to rule (and perhaps question the meaning of existence

itself), the facts of limit and finitude assume a central place in planetary perspective. To speak of earth as a closed ecosystem, then, is a rather stark reversal of the accustomed thinking of the human community over the last century, thinking which emphasized that the earth's resources were unlimited and basically at man's* disposal. And that leads to the second major point of this chapter.

ii. The complexity of relationships within our ecosystem.

> There it stood--
>   --a great tree--reaching
> Suddenly dark clouds formed--
>   lightning flashed--
>   --the life of a tree was shattered...
>
> The storm has spent its fury--
>   and disintegrated--leaving no clue
>   as to why this tree was struck...
>
> In its wake many lives must adjust
>   to that one moment
>   when lightning flashed--
>   and a tree fell...
>
> The birds that built nests in its limbs--
>   the insects that lives on its leaves
>   and in turn pollinated its blossoms
>   the flowers that grew to loveliness
>   in its shade
>   the owl that used it as a perch
>   to survey the countryside
>   the earthworms that lived in the
>   soil
>   and kept air around its roots...
>
> Even its natural enemies will know its loss.[20]

The ramifications of lightning striking a tree for this limited ecosystem, as captured by Gwen Frostic, illustrate in a dramatic way what we intend by the interrelatedness of all the components of any ecosystem in the biosphere, and, indeed, of the whole system itself. For these relationships prevail throughout the system, both among living things and between them and the nonliving environment. And their complexity can be gathered by the study of any particular ecosystem.

This in fact is the objective of ecology: "... how plants and animals interact with one another. What are the effects and limitations of the physical environment in relation to such processes as photosynthesis, nitrification, and organic decay?"[21] In this web of relationships one can discern a common thread of interdependency. We are, in effect, talking about a complex ecological system whose binding relationships are all-pervasive.

To conclude, when we reflect on the model (or metaphor) of system, closed system, and binding interactions within the system, the story of limitation--to be perhaps redundant--begins to ring loudly in human ears. It is the human component which thinks and speaks this story. Thus the third element in our narrative.

iii. Humankind as part of the ecosystem. The third aspect of our story-shaped approach to environment is the presence of the human species as an integral component in the biotic community. It is a significant reversal of traditional stories (at least Western cultural myths of the last several hundred years) to speak about the human group as being an element in the ecosphere. Now, however, whatever else might be said about the uniqueness of the human group in terms of reflection, language, and freedom, the story must begin with the emergence of the human group within the general context of planetary unfolding or development. It is not my intention here to defend evolution, since that, too, is another story (myth) of the origin of the planet. It does seem, however, at this particular moment of human experience that humanity's presence and general biological characteristics--if not also cultural--are both continuous with and related to all other species (however that human presence ultimately is explained).[22] The human presence is seen thus as singular both because of language and culture (enabling developments to occur broadly across the ecosystem), and because of the increasing density of human populations. These two factors, taken together, lead to increasing pressure being exerted on the environment. Finally, this ever-mounting pressure exerted by the human presence, when linked with the reality of the ecosystem as finite (limited, closed), threatens the balance of nature in ways that no other species ever has. And that leads to our fourth and last point.

iv. Delicate balance within the ecosystem. We have already spoken about the systemic nature of the planet, about the limited nature of this ecosystem, about the interrelatedness of its many and diverse component parts, and finally about the place of man* in nature. It remains only to point out the delicate balance within which all these elements in the biosphere, including man*, coexist and interact. The word "delicate" is chosen advisedly, since any significant intervention of any one species or force in the environment may produce a chain reaction which extends all through the system (the obvious contemporary examples of DDT and PCBs). Further, time and development have a way of threatening that balance. Humankind, for example, has existed quite harmoniously within the larger ecosystem for most of its history (two to three million years). Some time ago, however, perhaps about the time of the beginning of agriculture (and the 'new plow'), a direction was initiated which led to the gradual but drastic alteration of the ecosphere.[23] The rather rapid movement from agriculture to technology has significantly disrupted the balance of nature. The point of no return is becoming more and more obvious. And so we are back to the concrete experience of limit, restriction and constraint, the limit-to environment. "There is just so much usable water. Oxygen, minerals, and space for growth of whatever form, too, are measurable only in finite quantities ... We might ask how much longer, short of complete breakdown, the environment can sustain the pressures of use and the impacts of disruption that arise from expanding economies and the needs of growing populations."[24]

There appears to be, however, an unwillingness either to acknowledge the limit-to environment or, which is effectively the same, to live within limits. Perhaps this is where the parabolic-reversal dimension of story will gradually undercut the traditional myth. There are a handful of paradoxical phrases which seem responsibly to initiate the subversive, shattering process: "Small is beautiful," "energy is limited and expensive," "extinction is forever," "grow with less," "wildness is the state of complete awareness," "the power of renunciation," "do more with less," "convert waste into treasure," "true affluence is not needing anything."[25] I think perhaps a parable developed around the title, "Nature shall have the last word," might alert humankind to edges, limits and borders.

The point of such a parable, of course, is that humanity is free to--and capable of--intervening so dras-
tically and irremediably in the ecosystem that the
entire system would be rendered uninhabitable, not
only for humans but perhaps for most of the biotic
community. What we seem to find difficult to realize
as humans is that the human group is an integral part
of the larger ecosystem. The words of Chief Seattle
are remarkably poignant:

> The earth does not belong to man; man
> belongs to the earth. This we know.
> All things are connected like the blood
> which unites one family. All things
> are connected. Whatever befalls the
> earth befalls the sons of the earth.
> Man did not weave the web of life; he
> is merely a strand in it. Whatever
> he does to the web, he does to himself.[26]

This is what it means to say, "Nature shall have the
last word." Humanity can upset the balance of nature
irreparably, but ultimately the condition of nature
will affect us, since we are not "outside" the ecosystem. The human group may be able consciously to
imagine itself apart from (ex-sistere) the larger bio-
spheric environment, but, in effect, the impact of that
environment on them (smog, for example) is as certain
as their story about independence and domination. The
issue thus is rather about "interdependence," and
stories accentuating that dimension of humans-being-
on-earth would seem more adequately to portray human
experience at this particular time in cosmic--and
human--history. Here, however, we are beginning the
process of re-presenting, re-constructing and remythicizing, and that is the subject of the next
chapter.

   2.   Limit-of Environment

> But to have done instead of not doing
>   this is not vanity
> To have, with decency, knocked
> That a Blunt should open
>   To have gathered from the air a live
>   tradition
> or from a fine old eye the unconquered flame
> This is not vanity.
>   Here error is all in the not done
> All in the diffidence that faltered.[27]

66

If Ezra Pound, in the verses from Canto LXXXI
cited earlier,[28] challenged man's* exaggerated sense
of grandeur and his failure to acknowledge his limits,
here at the end of the same Canto he urges us on to
renewed effort in the face even of such limits. These
verses capture the sense of the re-constructing and remythicizing dimension of the theology of limit. In
other words, we have tried as accurately as currently
possible (story from ecological sciences) to state the
limits-to environment in order to show the limits-of
environment.[29]

Following our earlier analysis of the theology
of limit, we are here linking together the theology of
limit and the theology of story. There are two
reasons for this: first, theology of limit is related
to theology of story as parable is related to myth.
Theology of limit in other words exercises a critically
reflective function, checking and challenging the comprehensive and secure worlds that myth creates and--
more often than not--absolutizes (for example, "myth
of progress," "myth of one and catholic," etc.).
Theology, in fact, seems most fully operative and dynamic in challenging and subverting, since transcendence seems most fully possible at the moments of
crisis and the collapse of our myths. At the same
time, and this is the second way in which theology of
limit is related to theology of story, in the very exercise of its parabolic-reversal function the theology
of limit becomes disclosive of promise and possibility.
Theology of limit becomes partner with theology of
story in the re-construction and re-presentation of
human experience at the edges and limits--edges and
limits of environment in this case. Paradox and parable therefore not only subvert and shatter existing
worlds, but suggest in the very process alternative
worlds.[30]

In the first chapter of this part we saw in the
man-environment relationship a rather shattering and
sobering account of the limit-to environment. These
limits have been stated--in narrative fashion for the
most part--as earth's being a finite planetary ecosystem, containing limited essential resources of air,
water and energy, where all the component parts "dwell"
in a relationship of interdependency, where the balance
within the system is extremely delicate, and where,
finally, the human group emerges as part of the larger
biotic community in the ecosphere. In the face of such
stark limitations, nonetheless, the human group mani-

fests a strong tendency, to paraphrase Wittgenstein, to push and strain at the limits of nature/environment, but this urge points to something.[31] To walk right at the edges and boundaries is, as we have stressed, to create the possibility for transcendence and ecstasy. At the same time, in this disclosure of possibility at the limits and borders of environment, the same caution must be exercised as was counseled in pushing and stretching language to the breaking point.[32]

The urge particularly to thrust at the limits of environment has resulted, one might say, in three basic attitudes or stories about tha man*-nature relationship:

1.   Domination and mastery; ii. Conservation and Preservation;   iii. Stewardship and Earthkeeping.

i.   <u>Domination</u> and <u>mastery</u>

> The extraordinary patience of things!
> This beautiful place defaced with a crop
>   of suburban houses--
> How beautiful when we first beheld it...
> Now the spoiler has come: does it care?
> Not faintly. It has all time. It knows
>   the people are a tide
> That swells and in time will ebb, and all
> Their works dissolve. Meanwhile, the
>   image of the pristine beauty
> Lives in the very grain of the granite,
> Safe in the endless ocean that climbs our
>   cliff--As for us:
> We must uncenter our minds from ourselves;
> We must unhumanize our views a little, and
>   become confident
> As the rock and ocean that we were made
>   from.[33]

Robinson Jeffers has been called the "poet of inhumanism"; the poem cited here, Carmel Point, affirms vigorously the contrasting themes of dominion/ homocentrism on the one hand, and interrelation/ unhumanization on the other.[34] The fact is, however, that human history could be written quite authentically as man's* increasing "control over nature," beginning with the fashioning of the earliest tools that, with language, gradually distinguished--and indeed separated--man* from every other living species. Man's* is a history of subjugation: progressively harnessing the power and possibility of <u>wind</u> (sail, windmill), of <u>water</u> (water-wheel, irrigation) and <u>earth</u> (agriculture, minerals). Loren Eisely's description of the human presence is sobering:

> It is with the coming of man that a vast
> hole seems to open in nature, a vast
> black whirlpool spinning faster and
> faster, consuming flesh, stones, soil,
> minerals, sucking down the lightning,
> wrenching power from the atom, until
> the ancient sounds of nature are drowned
> in the cacophony of something which is
> no longer nature, something instead
> which is loose and knocking at the
> world's heart, something demonic and
> no longer planned--escaped, it may be--
> spewed out of nature, contending in a
> final giant's game against its master.[35]

Such in very broad strokes is the picture drawn from the story of human domination over environment.

What is at stake here is the "confrontation" between man* and nature. The experience of limits, as suggested in the first chapter of this essay, is understood in this story primarily as limitation, re-striction, barrier, and constraint. "Limited" (that is, limit-to) does not manifest disclosure, ground, and creativity (limit-of), but signifies rather defiant confrontation with hostile forces, breaking of barriers, and technical mastery over nature. The real contrast, then, is between limited and "limit-less." The goal of domination and an attitude of mastery are fostered by the story about man* as the center-piece of creation, that is, <u>homocentrism</u>. It is this story primarily which has pervaded the human community's self-understanding since the industrial revolution. It has technology as its metaphysics; it is utilitarian, manipulative and exploitative.[36] These characteristics are no more clearly captured than through the image of the modern freeway, as described by Denise Levertov in <u>Bus</u>:

> The turnpike, without history, a function
> of history, grossly
> cut through the woods,
>
> secondgrowth woods without memory,

> crowded saplings, bushes entangled,
> sparse weed crop on burned-over sandy
>   embankments.
>
> Brutally realized intentions speed us
> from city to city--a driver's world:
> and what is a driver? Driven? Obsessed?
> These thickarmed men
> seem at rest, assured, their world
> a world of will and function.[37]

As central perhaps in this poem as the utilitarian,
exploitative characteristics of mastery and domination
seen in the "turnpike," is the image of the "driver"
(driven? obsessed?), assured that his world is the
world.[38] Is this the posture assumed by the modern
technological superman?

    This myth of domination and mastery is not
readily open to parabolic and reversal modes of story,
since it is that very technology which has created a
world generally more commodious and comfortable than
humans had dared dream of. The debit side of the
ledger is only now being tallied, however, and the
cost of that convenience is slowly being assessed;
costs that, in terms of environmental impact, especially of essential resources, are literally staggering.
If understanding and care do not motivate humans to
reconstruct and re-present their story about them-
selves-in-the-world, perhaps selfishness--or, more
precisely, self-interest--will. Pushing at the edges
and limits of nature, then, through domination and
mastery, is destructive, both of nature and of us-with-
nature. The fundamental limitations of such a story
paradoxically are the limits of nature itself. Irresponsible straining at the limits of environment
radically upsets the balance of nature, and that dis-
turbance ultimately reaches man* himself: "Environmental exploitation occurs not in a void but in an
environment of which the exploiter is a relational
part."[39]

ii. Conservation and preservation

> I said there must be someway
> to determine
> what good
> a stalk of grass is--what

other measure but man?

In the hierarchy of use
to us
sea-oats are
inconsequential. But since

they exist, they
exist in the measure of
themselves
and promote the measure.[40]

A. R. Ammon's poem, Measure, furnishes an appropriate connecting link between the story of dominion and mastery, which sees man* as "the measure of all things," and the story of conservation and preservation, which affirms that, in the words of the poet, "things exist in the measure of themselves, and promote the measure."

Perhaps even now one senses something of a hollow sound to this story of conservation, since so much of the planet has been altered, and even ravished, in the development of civilization, particularly in the past century.[41] To talk, therefore, of conservation and preservation in our time is perhaps to suggest more an attitude or standpoint than to offer a comprehensive story about man* and environment. It is a sound and authentic viewpoint which might very well point the direction that such a story should take. To commit oneself, in fact, to conservation in the rapidly changing ecological context of the 20th Century is not only not anachronistic, but may even be essential to displace the contrary story of domination and mastery. We are coming to see, in effect, that not only is man not the measure of all things, but rather that even many of our highest technological--and seemingly humane--advances leave us with ambiguous feelings about their effects. Two obvious examples are advances in farming and medicine. Chemical fertilizers have increased agricultural production enormously, allowing us to feed millions more people; yet the effect of these same fertilizers on rivers and lakes and their ecosystems is devastating. The advances in medical technology are astounding and have remarkably lessened disease and suffering, but the jump in population that results creates an equally serious challenge, not to mention the many ethical problems resulting from the advances in biomedical technology. In this connection, William Barrett's reflections are to the point:

71

In cases like this, technology does not
seem like the alien monster of a horror
story, but very human indeed--ourselves
writ large. We seem to carry over into
technology that deepest and most vexing
trait of the human condition itself:
that our efforts are always ineradicably
a mixture of good and evil.[42]

The story of conservation on the contrary narrates and
portrays symbolically through forest preserves, natural
parks and other unique ecosystems that humankind has
much to learn from the complexity of the systems of
which--in not always obvious ways--they are a part.
Again the awe and reverence for natural systems seems
best articulated by our nature poets, and Robinson
Jeffers' De Rerum Virtute is particularly expressive:

One light is left us: the beauty of things,
   not men;
The immense beauty of the world, not the
   human world.
Look--and without imagination, desire nor
   dream--directly
At the mountains and sea. Are they not
   beautiful?
These plunging promontories and flame-
   shaped peaks
Stopping the somber stupendous glory, the
   storm-fed ocean?
      Look at the Lobos Rocks off the shore,
With form flying at their flanks, and the
   long sea lions
And the soaring hawk under the cloud stream--
But in the sagebrush desert, all one sun-
   stricken
Color of dust, or in the reeking tropical
   rain-forest
Or in the intolerant north and high thrones
   of ice--is the earth not beautiful?
Nor the great skies over the earth?[43]

In some ways, then, it is almost out of enlightened
self-interest that the human group bothers at all,
mustering even a degree of self-discipline and some
restraint on their own greed, to conserve natural
systems. Our separation from the natural world
generally leaves us with a subconscious feeling that
we need to keep in touch somehow with wilderness and
with the larger biotic community. I would call the

72

American saga the nature-civilization syndrome. The American ideal has always been pastoral--as it were. The return to nature. But as soon as we get there we either can't stand the utter silence and solitude, or we turn it into our basically urban habitat (litter everywhere and especially noise pollution from blasting stereos and other "home entertainment centers"). We cannot seem to make up our minds between nature (wilderness trips, nature hikes, summer homes, and even sub-urbs) and civilization (urban centers with all that that signifies).[44]

The story of conservation, therefore, though often belittled by the larger segment of society as the pet project of some "far-out" nature lovers, bird watchers, or other "eccentrics," is really an account of our own struggle for survival. In participating in the dedicated effort to preserve other living species and systems, we may indeed be developing attitudes and aptitudes essential to human survival. René Dubos quotes a California naturalist on this point: "The real importance of saving such things as condors is not so much that we need condors as that we need to save them. We need to exercise and develop the human attributes required in saving condors; for these are the attributes so necessary in working out our own survival."[45]

To conclude, the story of conservation-preservation is an account of man's* recognizing the limits of environment as creative contexts within which human possibilities are disclosed. Rather than perceiving the limits of nature as obstructions, restrictions and barriers, conservation sees such limits as manifesting significant, and even ultimate, dimensions of human existence. Indeed, in the conscious effort and struggle to cooperate and participate in the preservation and development of other living systems, humanity comes to appreciate its own synergism and mutuality with the whole living community. There is a sense, both authentic and ecstatic, in which communion with nature is creative of our fullest selves. Kenneth Rexroth captures this sense so forcefully in Precession of the Equinoxes:

> Time was, I walked in February rain,
> My head full of its own rhythms like a shell,
> And came home at night to write of love and
>   death,

73

High philosophy, and brotherhood of man.

After intimate acquaintance with these
  things,
I contemplate the changes of the weather,
Flowers, birds, rabbits, mice and other
  small deer
Fulfilling the year's periodicity.

And the reassurance of my own pulse.[46]

iii. <u>Stewardship and Earthkeeping</u>

The reassurance is
that through change
continuities sinuously work,
cause and effect
  without alarm,
gradual shadings out or in,
motions that full
  with time
do not surprise, no
 abrupt leap or burst: possibility,
with meaningful development
of circumstance...[47]

The sense of reassurance shared here by A. R.
Ammons in his poem <u>Saliences</u> seems to be an appropriate
mood for the story of stewardship and earthkeeping.[48]
We have allowed our reflections to roam rather broadly
and perhaps somewhat loosely over the first two stories
that create contexts for man's* responding to the
limits of environment, the story, namely, of domination
and mastery on the one hand, and conservation-preservation, on the other. The prior story in effect refuses
to cope with the reality of limits by an almost defiant
reliance on man's* limit<u>less</u> possibilities. The other
story, in virtually reverse fashion, gives full and
equal status to nature, that is, to the larger context
of the whole biotic community, affirming thereby that
the limits of nature are clear manifestations of the
necessity of living within (such) limits or, alternatively, of destroying the total environment.

The first story, of domination and mastery, reveals a destructive and care-<u>less</u> attitude toward nature, as Kenneth Rexroth reflects so poignantly in this
selection:

74

> The storm clouds rise up the mountainside,
> Lightning batters the pinnacles above me,
> The clouds beneath the pass are purple
> And I see rising through them from the
>   valleys
> And cities a cold, murderous flood,
> Spreading over the world, lapping at the
>   last
> Inviolate heights; mud streaked yellow
> With gas, slimy and blotched with crimson,
> Filled with broken bits of steel and flesh,
> Moving slowly with the blind motion
> Of lice, spreading inexorably
> As Bacteria spreads in tissues,
> Swirling with the precise rapacity of
>   starved rats. [49]

This scene, so starkly drawn by Rexroth, suggests a
story that denies all that is common and symbiotic between man* and the larger natural environment.

The story of conservation-preservation, on the
other hand, is deeply sensitive to the synergistic relationship between man* and nature, as shared by
Theodore Roethke in Journey to the Interior:

> As a blind man, lifting a curtain, knows it
>   is morning,
> I know this change:
> On one side of silence there is no smile;
> But when I breathe with the birds,
> The spirit of wrath becomes the spirit of
>   blessing,
> And the dead begin from their dark to sing
>   in my sleep. [50]

Nonetheless, by concentrating on the demanding effort,
to maintain ecosystems in their generally "undisturbed"
condition, conservationists can hardly devote the time
and effort necessary to alert the human group to the
inevitable impact that we are all continuously having
on the larger environment that "grounds" our organic
existence.

It is in this context, then, that a third story
is introduced into the repertoire of humanity's confrontation with the limits of environment, the story
of stewardship and earthkeeping. Gerard Manley
Hopkin's famous sonnet introduces this narrative
superbly:

> The world is charged with the grandeur
>   of God.
>   It will flame out, like shining from
>   shook foil;
>   It gathers to a greatness, like the ooze
>   of oil
> Crushed. Why do men then not reck his rod?
> Generations have trod, have trod, have trod;
>   And all is seared with trade; bleared,
>   smeared with toil;
>   And wears man's smudge and shares man's
>   smell: the soil
> Is bare now, nor can foot feel, being shod.
>
> And for all this, nature is never spent;
> There lives the dearest freshness deep down
>   things...[51]

Stewardship or earthkeeping challenges the human group
with the myth of simultaneously recognizing the limits
of nature and man*-in-nature, and yet straining and
pushing responsibly, cooperatively and creatively at
these limits as earth's primary steward and keeper.
The notion of stewardship goes back at least as far as
Plato and his observation in the <u>Phaedrus</u>: "It is
everywhere the responsibility of the animate to look
after the inanimate."[52] Further, as we shall see in
the next section, the book of <u>Genesis</u> also makes it
clear that man is to take care of the 'garden' (<u>Gen</u>.
2:15). The account of stewardship accepts <u>neither</u> the
despotic view of man* the dominating master over nature (even granted an inevitable measure of intervention in nature), <u>nor</u> the narrow conservative view that
man* should not modify nature at all (and still accepting the broader view of conservation-preservation
discussed above). There is a responsible middle
ground, this story suggests, which we have described
repeatedly in Wittgensteinian terms as thrusting cooperatively and co-creatively at the limits of environment. Examples of such co-operation and co-creation
abound; some of the obvious ones are sailing, natural
farming, animal husbandry, and similar instances of
care-ful designing of alternative eco-systems. The
notion of "gentle management" from A. R. Ammons'
<u>Meeting the Opposition</u> comes to mind:

> The wind sidles up to
> and brusquely in a swell flattens
> lofting one side
> of the spirea bush:

>   but the leaves have
>
>   so many edges, angles
>   and varying curvatures that
>   the wind on the other side
>   seeps out in a
>   <u>gentle</u> <u>management</u>.[53]

There appear to be two elements in the narrative of
stewardship and cooperation with nature which expand
and illuminate this story: first, nature as the
matrix or womb of human existence; and second, the
unique place which the human group occupies in the
ecosphere (language and reflection). These are somewhat delicate issues, so let's look at them more
closely.

a.   <u>Nature</u> <u>as</u> <u>the</u> <u>context</u> <u>for</u> <u>human</u> <u>existence</u>. It
is not necessary to repeat here what we have already
discussed, regarding the relationship between man and
nature and the evolutionary account. What needs to
be emphasized, however, is that in the story of earthkeeping and responsible stewardship the image of
humankind emerging from the process (as other species)
is central. The idea of sharing the 'stuff' of the
earth (<u>humus</u>) with all other species is illustrative
of humanity's dependence on "mother earth" (antidote
to <u>hubris</u>). Thus the sobering reflection of Charles
Hartshorne: "I am one of those who think that nature
would be, once was, and most likely will be again,
unspeakably magnificent entirely without man."[54] One
might want to question the concept of man's* absence
on hypothetical grounds, but nevertheless the paradox
is revealing. There was a time--indeed a long time--
during which the human group was <u>not</u> part of the
planetary scene. This did not in any way detract from
the beauty of that pre-human ecosystem. That raises a
question which leads to our second point: What has man*
added to the scenario and what has that addition
(evolution of man) meant?

b.   <u>The</u> <u>uniqueness</u> <u>of</u> <u>the</u> <u>human</u> <u>group</u>. The complementary side of earth-as-the-matrix-of-human-existence
is that humans brought a novel and--we (humans) are
wont to say--unique presence because of language and
reflection. Previous to the appearance of man* on
planet earth, things 'happened', instinctively and
deterministically, as it were, through the laws of
nature (natural selection, genetic mutation and
adaptation, survival of the fittest). What 'happened'--

even with the inevitable 'waste' that came as a by-
product of process or development--was, in our
language, immensely beautiful, and indeed independently
of humankind. With the appearance of humanity, however, a new element was added to the process, freedom.
Things no longer (simply) happened, but, more and
more, humans began to participate in the process, given
the particularly human characteristics of reflection
and language, in a way which was not possible--as far
as we know--for any other species. Here then one de-
tects a fundamental ecological transition, human freedom. Man* is able to intervene in significantly extensive ways in the process without always knowing--or
perhaps even caring about--the ramifications of his
intervention. The eminent philosopher, Charles
Hartshorne, sees freedom as the root of destruction,
suffering and evil in the world: "Man is the freest
creature, hence the most dangerous to himself and
others. This is what it is to be human. The great
opportunities of the human kind or degree of freedom
mean also great risks. Technology magnifies both opportunities and risks because it magnifies the scope of
the choices inherent in freedom."[55]

The story of stewardship and earthkeeping, then,
must keep these two realities, nature and society, in
a healthy tension. "Design with nature," is Ian
McHarg's creative synergy.[56] However the story is
narrated, the images, models and metaphors must be
chosen with care, so that both man's* relationship to
nature (as his originating and continuing matrix) and
his uniqueness (deriving from reflection, language and
freedom) in nature are yoked together in the common
enterprise of "building (co-creating) the earth,"
"restoring all things," "allowing Being to disclose
itself," or whatever the co-operative venture shall
properly be called.[57] A. R. Ammon's poem, One: Many,
sets the parameters of the task:

        To maintain balance
        between one and many by
             keeping in operation both one and many:

             fear a too great consistency, an arbitrary
        imposition
             from the abstract one
             downwardly into the reality of manyness:
        this makes unity
        not deriving from the balance of manyness
        but by destruction of diversity:

```
                    it is unity
                         unavailable to change,
               cut off from the reordering possibilities of
                    variety: ...

               not unity by the winnowing out of difference,
               not unity thin and substanceless as abstrac-
               tion

               out of many, one:
               from variety, an over-riding unity, the ex-
                    pression of variety...₅₈
```

CONCLUSION: In this second chapter we have discussed
the limits of environment as the context and ground
for living existentially and authentically in our
world. We saw three stories about possible ways of
responding to the limits-to environment: domination,
conservation, and stewardship. The first story, the
story of domination and mastery, is the one we have
been living for some time now in the industrial West,
but the impact has really just begun to be felt in
this generation--at least in any universe-al way. It
is an attitude that has been challenged by scientific
accounts, by the stories of philosophy and religion,
and most acutely by the poets of this century. The
second story is a quite ascetical and disciplined ac-
acount of man*-in-environment, accentuating the obliga-
tion to conserve and preserve the natural ecosystems,
since the mutuality of rights between man and all
other living and even nonliving elements, and the
future rights of posterity, dictate an attitude of
careful preservation of species, resources, and
habitats. The third and preferred story--at least when
narrated in conjunction with the conservation story--
recounts the saga of man* as steward and caretaker of
the planet. It mythicizes about the interrelationships
between humanity and nature as a cooperative venture in
which the human group, having emerged from the earth
(humus), represents the central thrust of that emergent
process--so far. Man*, therefore, naturally and necessarily is entrusted with the charge and challenge of
taking care of this small planet.

    According to the principles of our earlier method-
ology, we have generally described the limits-of
environment as ground and possibility disclosed in the
limits-to environment. Further, we have repeatedly
used Wittgenstein's expressive image of thrusting at the
limits of environment to suggest creative possibility

within the framework of rather stark limitations and
constraints. Man*, in fact, possesses and pushes at
the limits of nature positively and constructively
when he tests these edges and limits in a manner that
is co-operative and co-creative, moving <u>with</u> the
rhythms and patterns of nature. Thus, as we suggested
earlier, sailing, natural farming, and similar interactions with environment manifest healthy and fulfilling ways of pushing and testing its borders and
boundaries. We want to emphasize finally, as in the
experience of language-as-limit and language-as-
possibility, that the awareness of transcendence and
ecstasy seem deepest (highest!) and fullest at these
limits and edges. To live within limits, straining
cooperatively and creatively at these limits, is to
experience, in Crossan's words, "the joy of finitude
and the laughter of limitation."[59]

It seems, to sum up, that so much of what we have
been trying to capture in a re-presentative story about
man* and the experience of ecologic limits, has already been said much more powerfully over a century
ago by Chief Seattle of the Squamish tribe in a
prophetic speech delivered on the occasion of the
transferral of ancestral Indian lands to the federal
government. In quoting selectively, even though ex-
tensively, I hope not to lose the powerful impact of
his message:

> The Great Chief in Washington sends
> word that he wishes to buy our land...
> How can you buy or sell the sky, the
>   warmth of the land?
> The idea is strange to us.
>   If we do not own the freshness of the
> air, and the sparkle of the water, how
> can you buy them?
>   Every part of the earth is sacred to
> my people. Every shining pine needle,
> every sandy shore, every mist in the
> dark woods, every clearing and humming
> insect is holy in the memory and ex-
> perience of my people.
>   ... We are part of the earth and it is
> part of us. The perfumed flowers are
> our sisters; the deer, the horse, the
> great eagle, these are our brothers. The
> rocky crests, the juices in the meadows,
> the body heat of the pony, and man—all
> belong to the same family...

80

So we will consider your offer to buy
our land. But it will not be easy. For
this land is sacred to us.

The rivers are our brothers, they
quench our thirst. The rivers carry our
canoes, and feed our children... you
must remember and teach your children,
that the rivers are our brothers, and
yours, and you must henceforth give the
rivers the kindness you would give any
brother...

We know the white man does not understand our ways. One portion of the land
is the same to him as the next, for he
is a stranger who comes in the night and
takes from the land whatever he needs.
The earth is not his brother, but his
enemy, and when he has conquered it, he
moves on ... He treats his mother, the
earth, and his brother, the sky, as
things to be bought, plundered, sold ...
His appetite will devour the earth and
leave behind only a desert ...

There is no quiet place in the white
man's cities, no place to hear the un-
furling of leaves in spring or rustle
of insects' wings. But perhaps it is
because I am a savage and do not understand ... The Indian prefers the soft
sound of the wind darting over the face
of a pond, and the smell of the wind itself, cleansed by a midday rain, or
scented with the pinon pine.

The air is precious to the red man,
for all things share the same breath--
the beast, the tree, the man, they all
share the same breath. The white man
does not seem to notice the air he
breathes. Like a man dying for many
days, he is numb to the stench ...

So we will consider your offer to buy
our land. If we decide to accept, I
will make one condition: The white man
must treat the beasts of this land as
his brothers.

I am a savage and do not understand
any other way. I have seen a thousand
rotting buffaloes on the prairie, left
by the white man who shot them from a
passing train ...

What is man without the beasts? If all
the beasts were gone, man would die from
a great loneliness of spirit. For whatever happens to the beasts, soon happens
to man. All things are connected.
... Teach your children what we have
taught our children, that the earth is
our mother. Whatever befalls the earth,
befalls the sons of the earth. If men
spit upon the ground, they spit upon
themselves.
This we know. The earth does not belong to man; man belongs to the earth.
This we know. All things are connected
like the blood which unites one family.
All things are connected 60

3. Religion and Ecology

Both our present science and our present
technology are so tinctured with ortho-
dox Christian arrogance toward nature
that no solution for our ecologic crisis
can be expected from them alone. Since
the roots of the problem are so largely
religious, the remedy must also be
essentially religious, whether we call it
that or not. We must rethink and
refeel our nature and destiny 61

In the first two chapters of part two of this
essay, we have been describing environment and the experience of limit. Our methodology has been based
primarily on the theology of limit, according to which
we explored not only the limits-to environment, limitations both threatening and challenging, but also the
limits-of environment, especially conservation,
stewardship, and earthkeeping. The third and last
chapter broaches the question of religious language
and story, that is, the language and story adequate to
the limit-questions and limit situations encountered
in the man*-nature experience. As a general introduction to the religious dimension of this experience,
perhaps some reflections from the Tao Teh Ching, the
Taoist scripture, are appropriate:

There is a being, wonderful, perfect;
It existed before heaven and earth.
How quiet it is!

82

How spiritual it is!
It stands alone and it does not change.
It moves around and around, but does not
   on this account suffer.
All life comes from it.
It wraps everything with its love as in a
   garment, and yet it claims no honor, it
   does not demand to be Lord.
I do not know its name, and so I call it
   Tao, the Way, and I rejoice in its
   power.[62]

Although the man*-nature relationship may not be
as central in some religions as in others, since each
particular great World Religion has its own special
focus,[63] nonetheless every religion has stories de-
picting more or less elaborately man's* relationship
to environment, and so we will begin there. Then we
will move to possible modes of re-telling and re-
presenting these stories in ways which expand both
their metaphorical and analogical bases.

i.   Traditional religious stories about man* and
nature.

Perhaps this sub-title is somewhat ambitious.
So much research has already been done on the question
of ecology and religion that perhaps commentary rather
than research is more appropriate.[64] The general
thrust of this research is that, even though all cultures have, to one degree or another, intervened in
negative and destructive ways in their respective environments (in most instances learning from their mis-
takes and adjusting accordingly), nonetheless, whatever the tenor of its religious stories, the Judeo-
Christian tradition has been especially arrogant
toward nature. It is asserted further that such
arrogance is based upon their religion, that is, that
story, found in Revelation, which the Western tradition has shared over the last several millenia.[65]

It is not my intention here to rehearse this accusation, since it has already been argued and debated
for over a decade. Yet, I do think there are some
salient points in the debate which may contribute significantly to understanding the relationship between
religion and ecology. To begin, I think the exchange
between Lynn White[66] and René Dubos[67] best summarizes
the main features of the debate. White's article became the watershed for the extensive discussion on

religion and ecology which followed. His main thesis
was quite straightforward, and was contained really in
the title of his article: the historical roots of the
ecologic crisis are primarily religious. In other
words, to explore further into his thought, by religion White intends the overall perception that people
have about themselves and their world: "What people
do about their ecology depends on what they think
about themselves in relation to things around them.
Human ecology is deeply conditioned by beliefs about
our nature and destiny--that is, by religion."[68] That
perception in Western man was one primarily of domination and mastery over the world; therefore the religious story which grounded that perception must be indi-
cated. White then proceeds to prove his thesis, re-
lying on biblical evidence, especially dominiondom
from the book of Genesis (1:26), and the corresponding
theologies of man (body and soul) and nature (reality
to be understood so as to be controlled). White concludes by asserting that any reform in Western tradition must be religious, since the roots are so
thoroughly religious. Further, he rules out any solution from Eastern thought, given the radical cultural
divergence, insisting rather that the solution emerge
within the Christian tradition itself. Finally, he
finds a powerful resource there in the person of
Francis of Assisi and his religious philosophy of
conservation. White concludes: "I propose Francis as
patron saint for ecologists."[69]

     René Dubos, in reaction to White's sweeping
thesis, generally denies that "Western" man had a
monopoly on domination and dominiondom over environment, citing as proof examples from Egypt to China:
"All over the globe and at all times in the past, men
have pillaged nature and disturbed the ecological
equilibrium, usually out of ignorance, but also because they have always been more concerned with immediate advantage than with long-range goals ... If
men are more destructive now than they were in the
past, it is because there are more of them and because
they have at their command more powerful means of
destruction, not because they have been influenced by
the Bible."[70] Dubos continues in agreement with White
about the need for conservation, but rejects White's
simplistic solution of conservation, since human intervention in environments is inevitable. The more
realistic posture, Dubos asserts, is stewardship. He,
too, finds abundant examples of responsible stewardship
in Christian history, especially in the Benedictine

monastic history. Dubos concludes by offering as patron saint for ecologists St. Benedict of Nursia, founder of the Benedictine monastic tradition and its shining example of responsible stewardship.[71]

In a somewhat abbreviated reaction to both White and Dubos, I think several points ought to be challenged. First of all, though I think White's overall thesis is basically valid, that is, that Western man's* attitude toward nature is fundamentally one of domination, subjugation, and mastery, I do not think White can prove that that attitude is biblical. Although surely one can argue that the notion of dominiondom has its roots in Genesis (1:26), one must also acknowledge that the idea of stewardship is there as well (2:15), and indeed the New Testament suggests in several places the theme of restoration and renewal of all things in Christ (Rom. 8:22f; 1 Cor. 15:23). Neither is there solid evidence of any particularly harmful environmental attitude (beyond recognized interventions, especially agricultural) in the later medieval tradition. In fact, there is generally a sense in Christian medieval man* of God's overriding Providence and man's subservience to God. If man* is ever "lord" (master), he is always "lord" under God. As long as this religious sense of God and God's Providence was valid in Christian (Western) consciousness, mastery and domination were not really possible.[72] It is not the case, contrary to White's assertions, that Western man found his mandate to "subdue the earth" in the book of Genesis. Western man, rather, in the course of cultural evolution developed at some key point in his history a particularly arrogant character toward nature, and then used the book of Genesis, and related themes from Western Christian axioms (body/soul dichotomy; special creation of man) to validate the story of human mastery over nature.[73]

A word about Dubos' response. With respect to his generalizations regarding the universal ecological irresponsibility and recklessness of man*, I think one would have to acknowledge with White that there is something in the deep structures of Western culture which has led to the kind of dominiondom and ravishing of nature that particularly characterizes modern Western civilization. As David Crownfield notes: "Dubos points to the degradation of environment by many different peoples. But there is a difference between the destruction that derives accidentally from

85

ignorance and that which is the normal consequence of a basic attitude about life and the earth. The ancient Greeks depleted their land by accident; as soon as they understood what was happening, they adapted through development of a stable economic-ecologic system. Modern Western man, in contrast, has a basically exploitative, transient attitude about the earth which is inherently destructive."[74] I think this is the critical point. There is something deep in the Western psyche that creates this particular tendency toward irresponsible environmental attitudes. This posture, finally, is clearly religiously rooted, since it results from the total perspective that man has of himself in his world (a perspective dramatically portrayed, for example, by strip-mining). Dubos simply fails to deal with this problem.

To sum up, I think the accusation that the Judaeo-Christian story is synonymous with the story of domination and dominiondom, as proposed by White, is too simplistic. It is much more realistic to pursue the course taken by William Leiss in his The Domination of Nature, where he locates the domination-mastery syndrome in the gradual secularization of Western civilization. The key moments in this secularization process, he notes, are the Renaissance (mastery over nature through the natural forces) and the Baconian synthesis (yoking of science and religion to eradicate finally the effects of the original sin: religion restores moral innocence; science restores man's original mastery over nature).[75]

If it is true, we might add by way of postscript, that the Judaeo-Christian story is not necessarily an account of the dominiondom of man*, still there are some traditional doctrines associated with that story which make it possible for the domination-mastery account to be woven into the story. These are specifically the defined dogmas (in the Christian Conciliar tradition) of the origin of man* and the nature of man*.

a. Origin of man.* The answer to the question of human origins is that God created the soul directly.[76] This doctrine led in fact, whether necessarily or not, to the gradual image of a special creation and a unique creature. This has led to an exaggerated anthropo--or homo-centricity. Such an attitude contributed to the ideology of domination, since all other creatures are "under" human control.

b. Nature of man*. Closely related to the doctrine
of the direct and immediate divine creation of human
souls is the teaching, clearly defined as revealed,
that man is composed of body and soul, and that the
soul is (essentially) the form of the body.[77] It was
a logical step, and a vivid image, then, to read the
creation narratives as God's directly creating man's
body (from the earth) and soul ("infusing life"), the
body (in corresponding and metaphysical language) being
the matter (potentiality) and the soul being the form
(actuality). The yoking of creation narratives and
platonic philosophy--all scholastic efforts to the
contrary--led to the disastrous dichotomy between body/
soul, matter/spirit, earth/heaven. The practical result of all this was that the "real" world became the
world of the "spirit"; man's* true home came to be
seen as not here but hereafter. One has only to think
about the emphasis on "saving souls," "life of the
spirit," "spirituality," and so on.

The critical point, in conclusion, is that, although the Western religious tradition cannot be said
to contain any unequivocal doctrine of human mastery
over nature, nonetheless, given the development of
certain metaphysical assumptions, especially the body-
soul dichotomy (matter-spirit; earth-heaven) and homocentrism, a certain climate for human domination was
created. And so, when other cultural dynamics led to
the myth of mastery over nature, the traditional
religious story was re-told and re-presented as though
mastery and domination were essential features of the
originating narratives.[78] Perhaps we should conclude
with God's questions to Job:

> Then the Lord answered Job out of the whirl-
>   wind: "Who is this that darkens counsel
>   by words without knowledge?
> ... Where were you when I laid the founda-
>   tions of the earth? ... when the morning
>   stars sang together,
>   and all the sons of God shouted for joy?
> ... Have you entered into the springs of the
>   sea? or walked in the recesses of the deep?
> ... Have you entered the storehouses of
>   snow, or have you seen the storehouses of
>   the hail ...
> ... Is it by your wisdom that the hawk soars,
>   and spreads his wings toward the south?
> Is it at your command that the eagle mounts
>   up and makes his nest on high?"[79]

ii. Retelling the Story.

Earlier in this essay we described this function of the theology of limit as requiring two skills: first, an understanding of the rhetoric of narrative, that is, the rhetoric not only of the originating stories, but also of current fiction; and, second, an awareness of the metaphysics of religious belief, that is, the assumptions of the community creating stories-- and, thereby, worlds.[80] Let us pursue these two skills singly.

a. Rhetoric of narrative. We are talking here basically about the whole process of communication that transpires between the author and the reader.[81] If we apply that description to the biblical creation narratives, and their account of the relationship between man* and nature, we might conveniently settle upon the following summary: 1) Nature is not subservient to man*, but exists in its own right; it is 'good' in its own right and by its very existence blessed and praises God; 2) Man* is not just another creature, but holds a place of primacy in the creation narratives. At the same time that primacy is always exercised under the abiding Presence and Providence of God; 3) There is nonetheless a deep-rooted tendency of man* to covet center stage, even in defiance of God's power and presence. Man's* failure to recognize his place ('pride') leads to the spreading contagion of 'evil' (Adam, Cain, Babel, Flood ...); 4) There is all the while an overriding trust and confidence (amidst endless paradox, e.g., Abraham and Sarah's advanced age, sacrifice of Isaac, and indeed all the way to the Cross) that the purposes of God will be realized in ways that confound us, even though humanity is called continually to participate in God's promises and purposes.[82]

Robert Farrar Capon in Hunting the Divine Fox retells the story in contemporary narrative:

> And the Lord God took the man and put him into the garden of Eden to dress it and keep it. Look, Adam, he says, look closely. This is no jungle, this is a park. It is not random, but shaped. I have laid it out for you this year, but you are its Lord from now on. The leaves will fall after the summer, and the bulbs will have to be split. You may want to put a hedge over

88

there, and you might think about a gazebo
down by the river--but do what you like;
it's yours. Only look at its real shape,
love it for itself, and lift it into the
exchanges you and I shall have. You will
make a garden the envy of the angels.[83]

The biblical narratives, then, would fall under
the general fictions of conservation and stewardship,
as we detailed these earlier. One ought to note,
however, that the contemporary problem of nature and
society (man and nature) was not so acute at the time
of the originating stories. Clearly, the problem of
understanding man's* special relationship to nature in
such a way that the unique values of both nature and
society (environment and man*) are affirmed within the
relationship itself, is a relatively recent challenge.
Theirs, obviously, was a basic pastoral orientation
which, as well as accentuating man's* dependency on
nature, recognized his ability to manipulate and
manage nature's harvest. In contrast, for a large segment of 20th-Century urban humanity the tension between
rural and urban has not been pastorally resolved
(suburbia?).[84] Contemporary fiction, therefore,
struggles mightily with this central enigma of nature
versus civilization, called by Perry Miller the
"obsessive American drama."[85] In our earlier analysis
we saw the perspective primarily of some American
nature poets and their language of conservation and
stewardship; clearly there is a vaster fiction dealing
with this question.[86]

To conclude, one could re-tell and re-present the
Western religious story (at least up to the time of
the renaissance) authentically and convincingly along
the general lines of stewardship and earthkeeping,
accentuating the biblical basis of such stewardship
(wherein mastery itself is subsumed) as well as the two
major religious interpretations and traditions of both
Benedict of Nursia and Francis of Assisi.

b. Metaphysics of Belief. I think there are two
fundamental assumptions about the world and us-in-it
that are central to the traditional stories, namely,
1) The absolute sovereignty and otherness of God, and,
following from that the total dependency of all things,
including man, on God; and 2) The unique (special?)
kind of creature that man* is (under God). The difficulty with these two assumptions is that each of them
has, along with its positive and affirmative intent, a

negative and connotative side. First, the notion of God as sovereign and transcendent, along with the high purpose of accentuating creation as dependency and contingency, simultaneously created an unbridgeable gap between God and creatures, so that any hint of pantheism and animism was absolutely and rigorously excluded and censored. A natural tendency toward divine immanence (or transcendence downwards) was thwarted at every turn (finally, even God's own incarnation in Jesus was twisted and turned into divine consubstantiality). Otherness was indeed preserved, but immanence was lost.

Second, the uniqueness of man*, a generally obvious conclusion from his self-conscious reflection and language, and his propensity to story, led gradually to the exaggeration of "special" and ultimately to homocentricity and dominion. "Special" seems originally to have meant uniquely responsible because particularly favored. The traditional insistence upon the soul and the spirit as the essential component in the human make-up certainly preserved man's* particularity, or "specialness," but at the price of losing his oneness with the rest of created reality.

In sum, then, re-telling and re-presenting the religious story of environmental limits and human experience, we need to be aware especially of the following factors: First, the contemporary stories of conservation and stewardship, as forcefully articulated in modern fiction (especially poetry), are entirely consistent with the thrust of the original stories, even though the problem of society and nature is noticeably aggravated by contemporary ecological mismanagement. Second, the aberrations of dominiondom and mastery were later accretions to the story; they were drawn from the somewhat illicit union of medieval dogmatic formulations about the origin and nature of man* and a post-Renaissance legitimation of the scientific enterprise. Finally, the complex process of re-mythicization, that is, the transition from one myth to another through parabolic reversal, only signals to the theologian that this, too, is a story, and that the adequacy of the moment--adhocracy--ought not turn into fixed and rigid dogma (the story). As Crossan comments: "You have built a lovely house, myth assures us; but, whispers parable, you are right above an earthquake fault."[87] The lesson is obvious: as sound and currently adequate as our stories appear

to be--even the stories of conservation and stewardship, they are ours. Have we left room for transcendence, or God? That is, Do we recognize limitation as endemic, indeed making transcendence possible?

iii. Stories from other religious traditions.

There is a kind of fiction that exists in other
cultures which does not translate easily into our
language and stories, and some would say that that is
the case regarding man* and environment.[88] Any
cursory study of Taoism and its Japanese flowering in
Zen Buddhism, however, would seem to negate this
opinion. In fact, I would dare to say that Taoism as
an account of the man*-nature relationship is the
story par excellence for healthy ecologic responsive-
ness. Although it would take us too far afield to
validate this contention, nonetheless some initial
probings into the Taoist story are indispensable.

In Chinese (religious) history the intertwining
of the lives and messages of Lao Tzu and Kung fu Tzu
(Confucius) have symbolized a fascinating example of
the yang-yin complementarity itself.[89] Confucianism
accentuated the dimension of social harmony, that is,
accord within the human group (manners, customs,
ritual, propriety); Taoism emphasized the foundational
harmony between man* and nature. The fact is, however,
that social harmony was based on, and indeed derived
from, the more basic natural harmony.[90]

Huston Smith, with his usual fluent commentary,
characterizes the major thrust of Taoism as "creative
quietude" (wu wei), and describes this reality at
length in The Religions of Man.[91] I will be paraphrasing his description here. "Creative quietude
combines within a single individual two seemingly
incompatible conditions--supreme activity and supreme
relaxation ... It is life lived above tension (supple-
ness, simplicity, freedom)."[92] The Tao Te Ching,
traditionally attributed to Lao Tzu, and the Taoist
bible, as it were, describes this attitude as well:

> Keep stretching a bow, you repent of the
>   pull;
> A whetted saw goes thin and dull.[93]

And again:

> One may move so well that a foot-print
>   never shows,
> Speak so well that the tongue never
>   slips,
> Reckon so well that no counter is
>   needed. 94

Appropriately, water is the prototype of creative quietude: it adapts itself to virtually any surface; it holds incredible powers (floods, storms); it works apparently without working (gorges, ravines), and finally it is clearest when still. Listen again to the Tao Te Ching:

> Man at his best, like water
> Serves as he goes along:
> Like water he seeks his own level
> The common level of life
>
> What is more fluid, more yielding than
>   water?
> Yet back it comes again, wearing down the
>   tough strength
> Which cannot move to withstand it.
> So it is that the strong yield to the weak,
> The haughty to the humble.
> This we know
> But never learn. 95

This notion of creative quietude, finally, character-izes also--and especially--man's* relationship to nature:

> Those who would take over the earth
> And shape it to their will
> Never, I notice, succeed.
> The earth is like a vessel so sacred
> That at the mere approach of the profane
> It is marred
> And when they reach out their fingers it
>   is gone. 96

Perhaps the fullest contemporary expression of the Taoist vision is contained in Zen Buddhism. Zen training generally leads through three related pro-cesses, zazen (seated meditation), koan (problem or parable to show the limits-to reason), and sanzen (consultation about one's meditation) to the (intuitive) experience of Satori. The closest Western counterpart to Satori is the mystical experience (the

feeling of oneness with all things and the accompanying
ecstatic experiences). And yet <u>Satori</u> is really only
the true beginning of Zen training--everything else
being preparatory to it. "There must be further
satoris as the trainee learns to move with greater
range and freedom in the noumenal realm ... And in no
individual life (except perhaps the Buddha himself) is
it ever completely finished."[97] Huston Smith describes
four conditions which seem--though always inadequately,
he thinks--to characterize <u>Satori</u>, and again I am paraphrasing. First, life is good and the world is so
beautiful one can hardly stand it. Second, the dual-
isms of self and object, of self and other are totally
transcended. Third, the life of Zen "does not draw the
individual away from the world but returns him to it
with things in new perspective" (infinite in the
finite). Finally one is imbued with an "attitude of
total agreeableness."[98]

Taoism, then, when seen through the perspective of
"creative quietude" and of "satori" (in Zen), presents
an ideal of man*-in-nature which can serve to enrich
the Western Christian story of conservation and stewardship. Particularly illustrative of the Taoist vision,
finally, are the literature and art of China and Japan.
Both the <u>haiku</u> genre of poetry[99] and the fascinating
landscape paintings ("which place man in perspective as
a tiny observor of the vast universe--an observor who
is seeking to absorb himself therein") are illustra-
tions of the manner in which man* and nature are
closely merged and ever in communion.[100] Several <u>haiku</u>
from three Japanese masters furnish a fitting conclusion:

> Into the old pond
> A frog suddenly plunges
> The sound of water
>
> —Bashō

> A fallen blossom
> Is coming back to the branch.
> Look, a butterfly!
>
> —Moritake

> Pale simplicity
> Marks the arrival of spring—
> A pale yellow sky.
>   —Issa[101]

iv. Analogy and the philosophical contribution.

Earlier in our discussion of language and the experience of limit we talked about second level discourse, or explanatory-justification modes of story
(apologue and action).[102] The point made there, and
which I should like to apply here, is that there are
various modes of story. In the last several sections
of this chapter we have been dealing with myth and remythicizing, and particularly the myth of stewardship
and earthkeeping (myth in this case 'reconciling' the
complementary--if not contradictory--opposites of
society and nature). Now we should like to add the
stories of explanation and justification to that of
myth. There are two such models which seem to offer
further grounding to our experiential and revelational
accounts of stewardship and earthkeeping. They are
the Teilhardian model of "scientific phenomenology"
("hyperphysics") and the Heideggerian model of "Being
and technology."

a. Teilhard and scientific phenomenology. The reaction to Pierre Teilhard over the last two decades
has been (in his own neologistic way) "phenomenal."
There has been as much rejection of his apparent "too
facile pseudo-scientific systematics" as there has been
acceptance of his "comprehensive, imaginative, vision-
ary synthesis of the realms of religion and science."[103]
It is not my intention here to mount either an attack
on, or a defense of, Teilhard and his synthesis. As a
contemporary effort to validate the general story of
stewardship and earthkeeping, Teilhard's synthesis, I
think, is deserving of serious consideration. Given
the general caveats about the myth of evolution, about
evolution as inevitable progress, about progress
leading to utopia, and so on,[104] I am saying simply
that the phenomenological approach (letting things show
themselves for what they are) suggested by Teilhard has
some significant corroborating insights for the myth of
stewardship.

I am approaching Teilhard's phenomenology from the
perspective of the three dynamic processes which he saw
occurring in the evolutionary emergence of the human
group, namely, hominization ("peopling" of the planet),
socialization ("unifying" of the people), and
amorisation-personalisation ("personalizing" of the
union).[105] We will be exploring this threefold process and its implications for the story of stewardship
and earthkeeping.

94

1. Hominization: My synonym for Teilhard's neologism
in this case is "peopling of the earth." What Teilhard
is suggesting here is an alternative model for man's*
origin, and that model of course is basically evolutionary. The general sense here is that man* emerged
in the evolutionary process as the end-term of a continuous and complex development that can be traced
back--though not without significant lacunae--to the
origin of life itself. The advantages of this model--
and its accompanying images--are essentially two:
First, the traditional myth of the special creation of
man*, from which almost necessarily is derived the myth
of superiority, is reversed. Hominization as a description of human origins clearly relates the human
group to planet earth from which we have emerged (thus
the biblical metaphor, "The Lord God molded man out of
the dust of the ground"); at the same time the human
group is the first species to act reflectively (self-
consciously), to know, to speak, to ask questions of
meaning, purpose, etc. ("and breathed into his nostrils
the breath of life"). Secondly, the myth of homocentricity is also responsibly interpreted, since through
the hominization image the earth is seen as the matrix
--womb--of human existence, and the support system, as
it were, for everything human. The sense of the inter-
relationship of man* with all the components of our
ecosystem is tied into this image. Uniqueness is derived not from a special divine intervention (though
that metaphor is rich in symbolism), nor from some
other a-cosmic independence, but rather from man's*
place in nature. As Teilhard himself notes, man* is
evolution become conscious of itself.[106] Thus even the
man-nature dichotomy is suspect. Man* is nature
arrived at its reflective, self-conscious level.

2. Socialization. In the thought of Teilhard the
correlative of hominization, that is, the "peopling" of
the planet, is socialization by which he understands
unification of the people on the planet. This phenomenon strikes Teilhard as virtually self-evident: there
comes a point in time when hominization or peopling of
the planet, because of convergence and compression,
leads to the very issue of human survival itself. This
is the central thrust of socialization--humankind living
together in unity and harmony simply because disunity
and disharmony threaten human survival. Clearly,
species survival is a somewhat recent human concern,
since only recently has man* been able to imagine his
own extinction.[107]

One of the advantages of the model of socialization is that it describes man* primarily as a relational being, and thus rejects the metaphor of rugged individualism and self-definition totally and completely from within (for example, as composite of body and soul). This sense of relatedness and relationality helps to extend the concept of belonging already contained in the hominizing process. Man*, therefore, not only belongs to the ecosystem of which he is an integral part, his natural environment, "but man also belongs to his fellow human beings, across all barriers-- racial, sexual, economic, geographical, national and age."[108] The very notion of environment is thus enlarged and man's* niche further delineated (man = being-in-the-world-with others).

3. Personalisation-Amorisation. The third feature of Teilhard's phenomenology (phénomène humain) accentuates the process whereby unification within the human group (socialisation) must take place, namely, personalisation (or amorisation).[109] Teilhard insists that unification (convergence, synthesis) at the human level cannot take place in any fashion whatsoever, or, as he notes, haphazardly; such union, or unity, rather must simultaneously preserve and enhance the uniqueness (self) of each person in the union, and yet be a real and true union. His most common description of this process is "union differentiates."[110] Amorisation, then, responds to the question of how unification (essential for human survival) must take place if it is to be true union (not mere uniformity). To offer another of Teilhard's axioms: "Love alone is capable of uniting living beings in such a way as to complete and fulfill them, for it alone takes them and joins them by that which is deepest in themselves."[111] In other words, it joins them as "persons."

The value of "personalization" for the story of man*/environment is that it offers a viable and authentic alternative to the religious and cultural myths of rugged individualism, personal-individual salvation, and other egocentric destinies. The eschatological challenge in Teilhardian terms is the "future of mankind." "My" future is bound inextricably with the future of humanity. Self-actualization is really a cosmic and communal enterprise. At the same time, the question of survival necessarily involves the closely related issue of the "quality of life." It is a question really for the continued viability for evolutionary

development. The question is not just of human survival, but of the realization of the dynamics of the
process itself.[112]

To describe Teilhardian "hyperphysics," or
scientific phenomenology, in its particular application
to the issue of ecology, or man-in-environment, specifically, is thus to highlight three particular attitudes or vantage points onto reality: Man* emerges in
the evolutionary flow as every other species; man* is
not defined totally from within, but rather is essentially a relational being; and, finally, the significant reality is the future of humankind, a future defined as well by its quality (human, relational, etc.)
as by mere survival. It may seem, I should note, and
some have so accused him, that Teilhard is obsessed
with the place of man* and his future, and is therefore
a homocentrist concerned only with the future of
man*.[113] The fact is, however, that every aspect of
Teilhard's thought and meditation is shot through with
the profound awareness that man* lives in unity with
and dependence upon the larger context of nature that
everywhere surrounds him. It is obvious that the human
future is intimately tied in with the biosphere; any
significant disruption within the ecosystem affects
man*. There can be no either-or; only both-and.

To conclude, Teilhard's evolutionary model places
the human group within the flow of evolution. To
speak about uniqueness in Teilhardian perspective is to
talk about a unique trust and responsibility for the
unfolding of this process that man must assume because
of his unique qualities of reflection, language and
freedom. With the "appearance of man,"[114] things no
longer simply happen. Humanity participates in the
process--for better (and) or for worse--in an increasingly significant manner. Co-creation and co-operation
are expected, but not guaranteed. At best it is, in
Teilhard's descriptive phrase, a "groping toward the
future."

b. Martin Heidegger's 'Techne' and Technology. Perhaps we should say at the outset that Heidegger did not
approach the environmental question from the accustomed
direction of the scientific story which we have been
discussing. His approach rather, so characteristic of
all of his reflections, followed from his meditations
on Being.[115] And since Being is concealed rather than
disclosed (allowed to happen) in modern technology,

Heidegger sees technology as the decisively central activity in terms of which all other activities must be understood. According to one of his commentators: "There is therefore for Heidegger no possibility of comprehending or coping with technology from some vantage ground outside its own sphere of dominance. Everywhere in the modern age the Being of everything that is, is confronting man in the way that it does in technology."[116]

To deal briefly and responsibly with Heidegger's reflections on technology is a difficult challenge. I think, however, there are three central issues that need to be explored to even begin to understand Heidegger's discussion of technology: 1) Relationship between techne and technology; 2) Relationship between poiesis and techne; 3) Role of 'care'.

1. Techne and technology. The relationship between the Greek techne and modern technology, although nowhere fully elaborated in Heidegger's writings, is nonetheless the key issue in his discussion about the sacredness of environment. Greek techne is a focused knowing; that is, a mode of knowing which brings some object into being. It is not creation from nothing, since what is brought into being is already latent (potential) in nature (physis). Yet it requires human participation. As Heidegger notes: "Man's accomplishing is the knowing wresting of previously closed Being into what appears as what is."[117] The rather novel but radical contribution of Heidegger to the man*-nature interface lies here precisely. There is no sense in which man* masters Being from the outside. Man* himself is a being in Being. Through his techne (knowing that is doing), he creates something new, something, at least, really beyond what is already given. But the real meaning of creation here suggests "allowing" the Being of whatever is to become genuinely present (appearing). William Lovitt in his excellent discussion of techne and technology writes: "Thus techne in launching out beyond what is given and creating the work that gathers and lets appear, frees Being to happen decisively as unconcealment. It does so through attending upon and safeguarding Being by letting it endure powerfully in the work that has been brought forth."[118] Techne then is a continual process, since the pull of self-concealing of Being is constantly happening, even as self-revealing (unconcealment) is made to happen. Heidegger thinks that this pristine notion of techne existed only at the beginning

98

of western history and is fundamentally Greek (techne).

Then, following the radical revolution of values
deriving from what Heidegger describes as the Platonic
demeaning of natural objects and human products, and
the Aristotelian-Cartesian use of knowledge-to-master
(Renaissance), the pristine sense of techne has been
lost. In fact, techne has become modern technology
(technicity).[119] Being is masked and remains concealed
instead of being brought to light. "To represent this
masking, Heidegger uses the term Gestell. In it he
concentrates the sterile, mendacious connotation of
'scaffold', 'gimmick', and 'armature'. Trapped in the
technological Gestell, Being is not made radiant, it
is not housed, but, on the contrary, verwahrlost
('wasted', made 'tawdry', 'falsified')."[120] Heidegger
concludes that the gradual shift from techne to technicity, from 'vocation' to 'provocation', has made us
strangers on our planet; we are homeless. We are ruled
by the metaphysics of technicity, which is the conceal-
ment of Being. For this reason he calls for the rejection (overcoming) of metaphysics to save the earth.
The task is worth the effort, says Heidegger, quoting
Holderlin: "But where there is danger, there also
grows the strength, the agency of salvation."[121]

2. 'Poiesis' and 'techne'. Together with his discussion of the disastrous transition in the West from
techne to technicity, Heidegger also explores the relationship between poiesis and techne. Both terms
share the basic sense of 'making', that is, more precisely, 'making manifest', letting things appear in
their own nature. Poiesis or poetic thinking is a
'releasment towards things" (Gelassenheit zu den
dingen). It is the way of seeing all things as they
are in themselves. This is what Heidegger intends by
truth: disclosure of reality as it is (aletheia).
Techne, as we saw earlier, connotes the same kind of
'releasement toward things'. Just as poiesis is
authentic language (elemental and holistic vision of
the earth and the world), so techne is authentic work
(letting Being happen and revealing what-is in Being).

Applying the insights from Heidegger on poiesis
and techne to the experience of environmental limits
suggests an interesting and further comparison between
language and environment, a comparison drawn directly
from the relationship of poiesis to techne. Just as
poiesis connotes meditative thinking (besinnliches
denken) as opposed to calculative thinking (rechnendes

denken), so also techne suggests co-creation and vocation in contrast to technoligism which connotes mastery
and provocation. In sum, to think ecologically is to
dwell poetically;[122] to act ecologically is to work
technically (techne).

3. Role of 'care' in Heidegger's thought. "To be-in-
the-world in any real, existentially possessed guise,
is to care, to be besorgt ('careful'). Again, the
fundamental equation is anti-Cartesian: I care, therefore I am ... Care ... is the 'primordial state of
being' of Dasein as it strives toward authenticity
..."[123] Thus George Steiner positions 'care' (sorge)
in Heidegger's thought. It is in this sense that
Heidegger defines man as the "shepherd and custodian
of Being."[124] Care is the basic existential character
of being human. Understood as letting things be as
they are and appreciating their intrinsic value, care
uniquely describes the posture of poiesis and techne.
To care is both to dwell poetically and to work technically. Care suggests reverence in that it respects
the natural way of things-in-the-world. Care-ful is to
techne, in environmental application, as care-less is
to technicity and technologism.

To conclude, Heidegger's comparison between techne
and technology is a profound reflection on the direction modern technology has taken, a direction which
portends disastrous results, since man* has lost a
sense of Being and its manifestation. This loss has
only further aggravated the tendency to master and control. As Demske observes, quoting and commenting on
Heidegger: "Everything becomes fair game for the exercise of power; all beings are potential materials of
production. Thus 'the earth and its atmosphere become
raw material. Man becomes human material'; he is
merely 'the most important raw material'. There is the
frightening prospect 'that man will lose his self in
unlimited productivity' and become a mere functionary
of technology...."[125] At the same time, to understand
this process, and to realize that technicity has
brought us to the brink of ecological disaster, is also,
Heidegger insists, to affirm the possibility of change:
"But where there is danger, there also grows the
strength, the agency of salvation."[126]

v. Conclusions.

In the second part of this essay I have attempted
to apply the method and principles of the theology of

100

limit to the particular experience of environmental
limits. The first function of this theological approach is the obvious one of accentuating the reality
of limits and the limitation of story. As narrative
it parallels paradox and parable, challenging the existing myth. In the particular experience of man* and
ecologic limits, this demythicization or de-construction concides in fact with the contemporary story re-
counted by the science of ecology. We attempted to
broaden this primarily scientific account with the
creative approaches of other fictions also, especially
of representative American nature poets.[127]

Another function of the theology of limit, one
that parallels the theology of story, follows from the
response to the reality of limits-to environment. That
response, we discovered, leads to three different
stories about man* and environment. First, the myth of
domination and mastery, which effectively denies or de-
fies the limits-to environment, manipulating, managing
and mastering man's* surroundings and finally men themselves. The second response is represented in the myth
of conservation and preservation, according to which
man* stands virtually in awe and reverence before the
world of nature. The third account of man's* experience
of the limits-to environment emphasizes stewardship and
earthkeeping, that is, responsible interaction between
man* and environment. This account of man's* response
to the limits-to environment, I suggested, has all the
earmarks of a new (alternative) myth about man* and
nature.

The third function of the theology of limit addresses the issue of the traditional religious stories
and the possibility of their re-presentation and re-
telling. This function, we noted, has two foci: first
the rhetoric of the narrative itself and secondly the
metaphysical assumptions connected with the rhetoric.
Our reflections led through a re-presentation of the
Jewish-Christian tradition as very definitely a story
of stewardship and responsible care for nature, the
abberations of neo-platonic philosophy and the eventual
secularization of Western culture notwithstanding. At
the same time the incorporation of the Asian religious
story, as represented by Taoism and Zen, added a significant dimension--paralleling the myth of conservation
and preservation--to the Western religious narrative.
Finally, we offered two philosophical accounts
which appear to strengthen the myth of stewardship and
earthkeeping, namely, the scientific phenomenology of

Pierre Teilhard and the relationship between Being and techne of Martin Heidegger. The advantages of the Teilhardian perspective are derived primarily from the integration of the cosmic, living, and human phenomenon, downplaying in the process the dichotomies between man and nature. The unique insight from Heidegger's meditations is that techne ultimately is at the service of Being, and care for Being becomes the creative human challenge.

Through the whole process of re-mythicization, however, I continue to caution that this, too, is our story. Even as we live it and re-tell it, we remain open to its revision--indeed its reversal.

CHAPTER III NOTES

1. Ian L. McHarg. <u>Design with Nature</u> (New York: Doubleday, 1971), p. 5.

2. I use the word 'nature' and 'environment' interchangeably; they generally signify everything except man and that which obviously results from man's handiwork.

3. Robinson Jeffers. <u>Hungerfield and other Poems</u> (New York: Random House, 1954), p. 105.

4. The term 'man' here, of course, is used in the generic sense of human person. I have been affirming all along that language creates world; therefore, sexist language creates a sexist world. Thus care will be taken to avoid obvious sexist language. Since, however, so much in the following literature hinges on the phrase "man and nature," I will continue to use that phrase when I think it is appropriate, and I will asterisk the term man* when I intend it to be generic.

5. The term 'poetry' here is being taken as "an explanation in and with words." In this sense Annie Dillard's <u>Pilgrim at Tinker Creek</u> (New York: Harper's Magazine Press, 1974) is true poetry. See Warren Shibles, "Poetry and Philosophy," <u>Philosophy Today</u> 20:1976, p. 30.

6. <u>Tractatus</u>, 5.6.

7. We have discussed the issue of the primacy of language-as-limit various times in this essay.

8. See Edith Wyschogrod, "Death and Some Philosophies of Language," <u>Philosophy Today</u> 22:1978, pp. 255-265. See p. 256.

9. George Sefler, <u>Language and the World</u>, p. 191.

10. Paul Van Buren, <u>The Edges of Language</u>, p. 59.

11. Clearly, there is always a sense in which environment <u>is</u> our "life support system." 'Standing-outside' then means consciously, or in thought.

12. I am referring here to the modes of story discussed in Part I.

13. John D. Crossan, The Dark Interval, p. 14.

14. Canto LXXXI, The Cantos of Ezra Pound (London: Faber, 1957), p. 556.

15. Most of the studies which I am listing here deal more directly with the question of religion and ecology, but they do address the general ecological issues also. I am citing only the works that I used directly: Ian Barbour, ed., Earth Might be Fair (Englewood Cliffs, NJ: Prentice-Hall, 1972), and Western Man and Environmental Ethics (Menlo Park, CA: Addison-Wesley, 1973); William Blackstone, Ed., Philosophy and Environmental Crisis (Athena, GA: University of Georgia Press, 1974); John C. Cobb, "Christian Existence in a World of Limits," Environmental Ethics 1:1979, pp. 149-158; Clair Kucera, The Challenge of Ecology (St. Louis: The C. V. Mosby Co., 1978); William Leiss, The Domination of Nature (Boston: Beacon Press, 1974; Donella Meadows, etal., Limits to Growth; John Passmore, Man's Responsibility for Nature: Ecological Problems and Western Traditions (New York: Charles Scribner's Sons, 1974); and Paul Santmire, Brother Earth (New York: Thomas Nelson, Inc., 1970); David and Eileen Springs, eds., Ecology and Religion in History (New York: Harper & Row, 1974); Loren Wilkinson, Earthkeeping: Christian Stewardship of Natural Resources (Grand Rapids, MI: William B. Eerdmans Publishing Co., 1980).

16. Ervin Laszlo. The Systems View of the World (New York: Braziller, 1974), p. 14.

17. Ibid.

18. The Collected Poems of Wallace Stevens (New York: Alfred A. Knopf, 1955), pp. 320f.

19. Annie Dillard in Pilgrim at Tinker Creek (Harper's Magazine Press, 1974) has an imaginative account of this law: "The world has signed a pact with the devil; it had to. It is a covenant to which every thing, even every hydrogen atom, is bound. The terms are clear: if you want to live, you have to die; you cannot have mountains and creeks without space, and space is a beauty married to a

blind man. The blind man is Freedom, or Time, and he does not go anywhere without his great dog Death. The world came into being with the signing of the contract. A scientist calls it the Second Law of Thermodynamics. A poet says, 'The force that through the green fuse drives the flower/ Drives my green age.' This is what we know. The rest is gravy."

20. Gwen Frostic. Wisps of Mist (Benzonia, MI: Presscraft Papers, 1969), no pagination.

21. Clair L. Kucera, The Challenge of Ecology, p. 5. One way to discover the design of ecosystems, of course, is to study some. Kucera proposes a help-ful model representing the elements and their interrelationships:

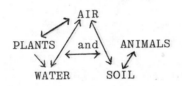

22. Huston Smith has a thought-provoking chapter on evolution and its verification as an account of the coming-to-be of the world (Forgotten Truth), pp. 118-145).

23. See Lynn White's discussion of the "new plow" in "The Historical Roots of Our Ecologic Crisis," Science 155:1967, pp. 1203-1207. See p. 1205.

24. Clair Kucera, op. cit., p. viii.

25. I cannot document the sources of many of these "slogans." As certain references, I can cite only E. F. Schumacher, Small is Beautiful (New York: Harper and Row, 1974) and Gary Snyder, Turtle Island (New York: New Directions, 1974), pp. 91-102.

26. See below, pp. 30+ for the full text of Chief Seattle's speech.

27. Ezra Pound, op. cit., p. 557.

28. Ibid., p. 556.

29. See David Tracy, _Blessed Rage for Order_, p. 117, n. 74.

30. Although the new story (myth) is inevitably fore-shadowed in the de-construction (parable), I would not want to sacrifice the power of parable to the desire for re-construction.

31. See above, Part II, 2, iii.

32. Paul Van Buren, _Edges of Languages_, p. 83.

33. Robinson Jeffers, _op. cit._, p. 97.

34. See Arthur Coffin, _Robinson Jeffers: Poet of In-humanism_ (Madison, WI: University of Wisconsin Press, 1971).

35. Loren Eisley, _The Firmament of Time_ (New York: Athenaeum, 1971), p. 123f.

36. See William Leiss, _The Domination of Nature_, Chapter 3.

37. Denise Levertov, _The Freeing of the Dust_ (New York: New Directions, 1975), p. 4.

38. One is reminded of Sinclair Lewis' (_Main Street_) characterization of the folks on the Main Street of Gopher Prairie: "A savorless people, gulping tasteless food, and sitting ... coatless and thoughtless, in rocking chairs, listening to mechanical music saying mechanical things ... and viewing themselves as the greatest race in the world."

39. See Peter A. Y. Gunter, "The Big Thicket," in _Philosophy and Environmental Crisis_, p. 134.

40. A. R. Ammons. _Diversifications: Poems_ (New York: W. W. Norton & Co., 1974), p. 19. Anyone who's been to the seashore knows the further value of sea-oats.

41. This, of course, is not to assert that interven-tion and destruction did not happen earlier. It's just that the process has accelerated in the last half-century or so. See René Dubos, _A God Within_ (New York: Scribners, 1972), p. 161.

42. William Barrett, The Illusion of Technique, p. 20.

43. Robison Jeffers, op. cit., p. 95.

44. See Lee Marx, "Pastoral Ideals and City Troubles," Western Man and Environmental Ethics, pp. 93-115.

45. Quoted by René Dubos, op. cit., p. 167.

46. Kenneth Rexroth. The Phoenix and the Tortoise (New York: New Directions, 1944), p. 56.

47. A. R. Ammons. The Selected Poems: 1951-77 (New York: W. W. Norton & Co., 1977), p. 49.

48. I have appropriated the term "earthkeeping" from Loren Wilkinson, ed., Earthkeeping: Christian Stewardship of Natural Resources.

49. Kenneth Rexroth, op. cit., p. 67.

50. Collected Poems of Theodore Roethke (New York: Doubleday-Anchor, 1975), p. 189.

51. Poems and Prose of Gerard Manley Hopkins (London: Penguin Books, 1953), p. 27.

52. Quoted in John Passmore, Man's Responsibility for Nature, p. 28.

53. A. R. Ammons, Diversifications, p. 16. Emphasis is mine.

54. Cited in John Bennett, "A Context for the Land Ethic," Philosophy Today 20:1976, 124-133. See p. 132, n. 32. One is reminded in this context of Robinson Jeffer's powerful poem, "Their Beauty Has More Meaning," in The Double Axe and Other Poems (New York: Liveright, 1977), p. 120.

> Yesterday morning enormous the moon hung
>   low on the ocean,
> Round and yellow-rose in the glow of dawn;
> The night-herons flapping home were down on
>   their wings.
>   Today.
> Black is the ocean, black and sulphur the
>   sky.
> And white seas leap. I honestly do not
>   know which day is more beautiful.

I know that tomorrow or next year or in
   twenty years
I shall not see these things--and it does
   not matter, it does not hurt;
They will be here. And when the whole
   · human race
Has been like me rubbed out, they will
   still be here: storms moon and ocean,
Dawn and the birds. And I say this: their
   beauty has more meaning
Than the whole human race and the race of
   birds.

55. Charles Hartshorne, "The Environmental Results of Technology," in Philosophy and Environmental Crisis, p. 78.

56. Op. cit. Wendell Berry makes the point well: It (nature, poetry) seeks to give us a sense of our proper place in the scheme of things ... Man, it keeps reminding us, is the centre of the universe only in the sense that wherever he is it seems to him that he is at the center of his own horizon; the truth is that he is only a part of a vast complex of life, on the totality and the order of which he is blindly dependentl." "A Secular Pilgrimage," in Western Man and Environmental Ethics, p. 141.

57. Phrases lifted obviously from Teilhard de Chardin, St. Paul (Romans), and Martin Heidegger.

58. A. R. Ammons, The Selected Poems, 1951-77, pp. 38f.

59. John Crossan, The Dark Interval, p. 17f.

60. Cited in The Power of the People: Active Non-Violence in the United States, ed. by Robert Cooney and Helen Michalowsky (Culver City, CA: Peace Press, 1977), p. 6f.

61. Lynn White, Jr., "Historical Roots of Our Ecologic Crisis," p. 1207.

62. Cited in K. L. Reichelt. Meditation and Piety in the Far East (New York: Harper and Row, 1954), p. 41.

63. See T. Patrick Burke, The Reluctant Vision (Philadelphia: Fortress, 1974), Chapter 1.

64. See bibliography listed above, n. 15.

65. I am using the word 'western' here with the general qualification that it applies primarily to the industrial nations of the West.

66. Lynn White, art. cit.

67. René Dubos, A God Within, pp. 153-174.

68. Lynn White, art. cit., p. 1205.

69. Ibid., p. 1207.

70. René Dubos, op. cit., pp. 161f.

71. Ibid., p. 164f.

72. See William Leiss, The Domination of Nature, pp. 29ff.

73. For a response to White on this point, see J. Patrick Dobel, "Stewards of the Earth's Resources," Christian Century 94:1977, pp. 906-909.

74. David Crownfield, "The Curse of Abel: An Essay in Biblical Ecology," The North American Review, Summer: 1973, p. 63.

75. William Leiss, op. cit., pp. 35-71.

76. Pope Pius XII, Humani Generis (Encyclical Letter): "That souls are immediately created by God is a view which the Catholic Faith imposes on us." In The Church Teaches (St. Louis: Herder, 1960), p. 154.

77. Council of Vienne (1311-1312): "We define that, whoever presumes to assert, defend, or stubbornly hold that the rational soul is not of its own nature and essentially the form of the body, is considered to be a heretic." In The Church Teaches, p. 147.

78. And so, for example, subsequent to the Renaissance and Francis Bacon's synthesis, we read in a proposed schema from Vatican Council I: "God was intend on making man to his own image and likeness. That man might have dominion over the entire earth. God breathed the breath of life into the body that he formed from the dust of the earth ... " Ibid., p. 150.

79. Job, 38-39, passim.

80. See above, Part II, in our discussion of theology of limit and theology of story.

81. See Wayne Booth, The Rhetoric of Fiction (Chicago: University of Chicago Press, 1961), Preface.

82. The New Testament is generally consistent with the Old Testament in its overall approach to these four themes. For a comprehensive treatment of biblical themes in ecology, see Paul Santmire, Brother Earth, pp. 80f.

83. Cited in Earthkeeping: Christian Use of Natural Resources, p. 255.

84. See Leo Marx, "Pastoral Ideals and City Troubles," in Western Man and Environmental Ethics, pp. 93-115.

85. Perry Miller. Errand into the Wilderness (Cambridge, MA: Belknap Press, 1962), p. 204.

86. See J. Ronald Engel, "The 'New Primitivism'," in Belonging and Alienation, Philip Hefner and Widdick Schroeder,eds. (Chicago, CSSR, 1975), pp. 33-64. See, also, Annie Dillard, Pilgrim at Tinker Creek (Harper's Magazine Press, 1974).

87. John D. Crossan, The Dark Interval, p. 57.

88. See Lynn White, art. cit., p. 1206.

89. See Laurence G. Thompson, Chinese Religion: An Introduction (Encino, CA: Dickenson, 1975), pp. 3f.

90. Ibid., p. 7: "In an integrated universe, it will occur to men to seek out the signs writ large in nature whereby they may confirm that human actions are in accord or discordant with the tao of this universe... "

91. Huston Smith. The Religions of Man (New York: Harper, 1965), pp. 204f.

92. Ibid., p. 204.

93. Cited in Huston Smith, op. cit., p. 205.

94. Ibid.

95. Ibid.

96. Ibid.

97. Ibid., pp. 149-150.

98. Ibid., p. 151.

99. "A Haiku is not a poem, it is not literature; it is a hand beckoning, a door half-opened, a mirror wiped clean. It is a way of returning to nature ... " Quoted by Wendell Berry, "A Secular Pilgrimage," in Western Man and Environmental Ethics, p. 149.

100. See Laurence Thompson, op. cit., p. 7.

101. One Hundred Famous Haiku. Selected and translated by Daniel C. Buchanan (San Francisco: Japan Publications, Inc., 1973), pp. 88, 40, 32.

102. See above, Part II, theology of story.

103. The bibliography on Teilhard is extensive. In fact, to cite Huston Smith, "We know of no other twentieth-century thinker who has an entire journal devoted to the propagation of his theses." Further, a new surge in Teilhardian study has been sparked by the 100th anniversary of his birth (1881-1981).

104. The story of evolution has its own particular methodological problems, especially the problem of verification. Huston Smith strongly criticizes evolution as the last prop for the hope (not the fact) of progress (forward). See Forgotten Truth: The Primordial Tradition, pp. 121-145.

105. Teilhard's neologisms are not necessary to my critique. I use them because they are so much a part of his narrative.

106. Phenomenon of Man (New York: Harper and Row, 1965), p. 221.

107. There was always the possibility that God might annihilate the whole human project (though it seemed contrary to Providence), but it was never imaginable that man* could destroy himself total-ly. Species destruction seems to be a relatively new spectre following the control over nuclear power.

108. Philip Hefner, "Foundations of Belonging," in Belonging and Alienation, p. 162.

109. Phenomenon of Man, p. 262.

110. Ibid., p. 265.

111. Ibid.

112. Given the spectres of Huxley's Brave New World and Orwell's 1984, we have become accustomed to speak not only of human survival, but also--and maybe especially--of the improvement of the quality of life.

113. See Paul Santmire, Brother Earth, p. 108.

114. Pierre Teilhard de Chardin. The Appearance of Man (New York: Harper & Row, 1966).

115. See George Steiner, Martin Heidegger (New York: Viking Press, 1978), p. 36.

116. William Lovitt, "Techne and Technology," Philoso-phy Today 24:1980, pp. 62-72. See p. 63.

117. Martin Heidegger, Introduction to Metaphysics. Translated by Ralph Manheim (New York: Doubleday,

1961), p. 134.

118. William Lovitt, art. cit., p. 65.

119. Since techne is probably best translated "technology," some other word is necessary to describe modern technology, such as, "technicity," "technologism," etc.

120. George Steiner, op. cit., p. 139.

121. Quoted by George Steiner, op. cit., p. 141.

122. This is the poet Holderlin's phrase which so affected Heidegger. As Steiner noted: "The fatality of technicity lies in the fact that we have broken the links between techne and poiesis. It is time we turned to the poets." Ibid.

123. Ibid., p. 101.

124. See John Dunne's comment in The Way of All The Earth (New York: Macmillan, 1972), p. 68.

125. James M. Demske. Being, Man, and Death (Lexington KY: University of Kentucky, 1970), p. 136.

126. See above, note 121.

CHAPTER IV

DEATH AND THE EXPERIENCE OF LIMITS

> There is a line in Verlaine I shall not
>   recall again,
> There is a street close by forbidden to
>   my feet,
> There's a mirror that's seen me for the
>   very last time,
> There is a door that I have locked till
>   the end of the world.
> Among the books in my library (I have
>   them before me)
> There are some that I shall never open
>   now.
> This summer I complete my fiftieth year;
> Death is gnawing at me ceaselessly.
>
>   -Jorge Luis Borges, Limits[1]

The third dimension of our essay on the religious experience of limits, and the corresponding theology of limit, is death. Before exploring the implications of the limit-experience of death, however, two preliminary observations are necessary. I want first to review the limit situation of death in relation to the two limit-experiences already discussed, namely, language and environment. The second observation deals with the issue of methodology, that is, the application of the principles of the theology of limit to death-as-limit.

Death lends itself quite readily to both the general and the specific reflections on limits that we have already encountered in both the limits of language and the limits of environment. Death, just as certainly as language and environment, manifests a comprehensive context within which--and toward which--life is lived. In this sense the continuity of death with language and environment as limit-experiences is apparent; they--all three--mark the well-defined confines, boundaries and borders (horizons) within which human existence is spent. As with the experience of language ("the limits of my language are the limits of my world"), and the experience in environment ("Nature will have the last word"), there is a sense of absoluteness also to the limits of death, as John Dunne captures so well in his Cartesian-style metaphor, "I am and I shall die."[2]

115

At the same time, however, that we draw out the similarities among language, environment, and death as contexts within which humanity experiences uniquely the reality of limits, we note that death confronts the human person existentially with the reality of limits in a way that language and environment generally do not.[3] In fact, from what we have already discovered in our reflections on language and environment, it seemed that the experience of limits was not immediately evident, but was discernible rather in the self-conscious reflection on language (How get outside of language?) and environment (Humans alone ex-sist, that is, consciously stand apart from nature). Such does not seem to be the case in the event of death, since death works certainly and continuously at the level of the subconscious (or more accurately, the unconscious). There is an innate awareness in us all that we are mortal. In fact, it seems that much of our contemporary culture is designed to deny or at least evade this gnawing awareness. As A. R. Ammons reminds us in one of his characteristic aphorisms: "odd that/death the evidence/for which is/absolute/is completely/incredible/eath of us/exception's single."[4]

The second preliminary observation addresses the issue of methodology, that is, the concrete application of the principles of the theology of limit to the limit-situation particularly of death. As we have suggested earlier, the primary objective of the theology of limit is to alert us to the limit-situations and limit-questions of human experience. This objective is further specified by the two critical dimensions of limit and their related functions: limit-to-experience, that is, the parabolic-paradoxical-reversal function of de-construction and de-mythicization, and limit-of experience, the mythical-integrative function of re-construction and re-presentation. In the application of these functions of the theology of limit to the limit-situation of death, we will be exploring three specific issues: 1) Death as limit-to human existence; 2) Death as limit-of life; 3) Religious Stories and Death.

1. DEATH AS LIMIT-TO HUMAN EXISTENCE

> Death. Nothing is simpler. One is dead.
> The set face now will fade out; the bare
>   fact,

Related movement, regular, intact,
Is reabsorbed, the clay is on the bed.
The soul is mortal, nothing: the dim
   head
On the pillow, less. But thought
   clings flat
To this, since it can never follow that
Where no precision of mind is bred.

Nothing to think of between you and All!
Screaming processionals of infinite
Logic are grinding down receding cold!
O fool! Madness again! Turn not, for it
Lurks in each pointless cranny, and you
   sprawl
Blurring a definition. Quick!. you are
   old.

              -Yvor Winters, <u>The Realization</u>[5]

   If it was difficult to grasp the meaning of the
limits of <u>language</u>, and only slightly less difficult
to comprehend the reality of <u>ecologic limits</u>, there is
an even thornier problem with the reality of death.
On the one hand, there is the rather complex position
which asserts that no person is able to grasp the
reality of his or her own death. Freud is the primary
spokesman for this standpoint:

          Our own death is indeed <u>unimaginable</u>
          and whenever we make an attempt to imagine
          it we can perceive that we really survive
          as spectators. Hence the psychoanalytic
          school could venture the assertion that at
          bottom <u>no one believes in his own death</u>,
          or to put it another way, in the un-
          conscious every one of us is convinced of
          his own immortality.[6]

It appears, then, that we may not be able really to
grasp the limit-to dimensions of death. As Wittgenstein notes also in this regard: "Death is not an
event in life: we do not live to experience death...
Our life has no end just as our visual field has no
limit."[7] The precise problem here is quite differently
perceived by Freud than by Wittgenstein. Freud says
quite simply that we cannot imagine ourselves <u>dead</u>; we
really survive as spectators. Wittgenstein on the
other hand connects death and language in an imagina-

                          117

tive way. Just as one cannot find a vantage point outside of language with which to take the measure of
language, so one cannot find a perspective beyond
death to speak about death. Just as "the limits of my
language are the limits of my world," so with death
the individual's world comes to an end--one no longer
speaks a language.[8] Death for Wittgenstein, then, "is
not an event in life. It is not a fact of the world."[9]
Death is the limit of my world not in the sense of
being part of the world, but rather that through it my
world comes to an end. "To speak of something beyond
this limit as if my ordinary language could be used is
not even to speak important nonsense."[10] For this
reason Wittgenstein denies the possibility of _saying_
anything at all about death. This does not mean of
course that language cannot "point to" or "show" anything; and we are back to Wittgenstein's philosophy of
religious language: "The tendency to thrust at the
limits of language points to something."[11]

In sum, although Freud's approach (psychological)
is obviously different from Wittgenstein's (linguistic),
nonetheless they both accentuate the difficulty of describing death-as-limit-to life. They do not disagree
about the rock-bottom signification of death as the
cessation of bodily processes (biological death), but
rather about what that means to the subject (person)
and his language (story).

The second aspect of the problem of coming to
grips with the reality of death as limit-to life is
the social context within which the stories of death
are narrated. If it is difficult for the individual
to imagine his own immortality, that is, to grasp the
real sense in which his world ends, whether from a
psychological or a linguistic perspective, that difficulty is aggravated by the social matrix--at least
of our twentieth century technocratic society. There
is an almost systematic attempt in society to evade,
avoid and repress the reality of death. Despite the
spate of courses in thanatology and the heightened
media interest in death and dying over the last decade
or so, one still feels something like the child in
Emily Dickinson's poem:

> I noticed people disappeared
> When but a little child--
> Supposed they visited remote,
> Or settled regions wild.

> Now know I they both visited
> And settled regions wild,
> But did because they died,--a fact
> Withheld the little child.[12]

There is an unconscious avoidance mechanism at work in the society at large closely paralleling the individual denial of death described by Freud. This process of denial is endemic to a highly developed technological society, since that society has prized itself on the ability to control, manipulate, manage, operate and dominate. But... death is the ultimate controller. It cannot be controlled, managed and dominated. And so it is avoided.[13]

We are attempting to carry on a discussion about death as limit-to life, then, in the uninviting context of _both_ the individual's difficulty imagining death as finality, _and_ of the social process of avoidance and repression of death. It is no wonder our stories about death deny the reality of death, or repress it, or avoid it.[14] Even our religious stories, though admitting psychological-biological death, nonetheless turn attention away from the full reality of death (as end, finality, termination), and toward an eternal existence in a more or less modified corporeal form. The task of de-construction and de-mythicization, therefore, must push ahead in the face of strong resistance both from the individual and his unshakeable reluctance to suspend belief in a _state-after death_ (if there is one) and focus on the _fact_ of death; and at the same time from the society and its systematic shying away from confrontation with mortality (embalming, primping-up of the corpse, comfort coffins, indestructable vaults, and all the way to cryonics).[15]

Perhaps the best way for the theology of limit to accomplish its primary task of accentuating death as limit-to life, and thereby to reverse the attitudes of denial and evasion, is to approach the _fact_ of death from the perspectives of biology, of psychology, and of philosophy. An examination of these three particular stories, shot through where possible with poetic insight, might achieve the parabolic-reversal function that we are after here.

1. BIOLOGICAL DEATH. Medical science has struggled for years to define death in concrete physiological terms. The task of course is complicated because it assumes that one has a clear definition of life. In

119

the past century the definition of death has shifted
gradually from heart-related functions to cerebral-
related functions in the same way that the notion of
human life has found its focus moved from heart to
head.[16]   Robert Veatch in a rather creatively eclectic
fashion suggests the following medical-biological de-
finition/determination of death:

> A person will be considered dead if in
> the announced opinion of a physician,
> based on the ordinary standards of
> medical practice, he has experienced an
> irreversible cessation of spontaneous
> respiratory and circulatory functions.
> In the event there is reason to believe
> that cerebral functions have ceased
> while spontaneous respiratory and cir-
> culatory functions remain, a person
> will be considered dead if in the an-
> nounced opinion of a physician, based
> on ordinary standards of medical prac-
> tice, he has experienced an irreversible
> cessation of spontaneous cerebral func-
> tions. Death will have occurred at the
> time when the relevant functions ceased.
>   It is provided, however, that no per-
> son shall be considered dead even with
> the announced opinion of a physician
> solely on the basis of an irreversible
> cessation of spontaneous functions if he.
> while competent to make such a decision,
> has within the limits of reasonableness
> explicitly rejected the use of this
> standard or, if he has not expressed
> himself on the matter while competent,
> his legal guardian or next of kin ex-
> plicitly expresses such rejection.
>   It is further provided that no physic-
> ian shall pronounce the death of any
> individual in any case where there is
> significant conflict of interest with
> his obligation to serve the patient
> (including commitment to any other
> patients, research, or teaching pro-
> grams which might directly benefit from
> pronouncing the patient dead).[17]

The effort at such precision in the determination of
death is no longer--if it really ever was--merely
theoretical, or even just broadly practical (record-

keeping, and so forth). The eminently pragmatic
character of the determination of death is tied to the
possibility of organ transplants. Such medical intervention can only follow upon the legal determination
of death, and the law in this case generally follows
the accepted medical determination. Veatch manages in
his description of death to incorporate all of the
criteria currently accepted by the medical profession.
At the same time he acknowledges the possibility that
cerebral functions may have ceased while spontaneous
respiratory activity and circulatory functions continue (the case with Karen Quinlan), and therefore
freedom of choice (within reasonable limits) is
guaranteed the person (or their legal guardian) in
determining death. Veatch emphasizes finally that
provisions be made to eliminate any conflict of
interest (on the part of those determining the fact of
death).[18]

ii. PSYCHOLOGICAL DEATH

> Invention sleeps within a skull
> No longer quick with light,
> The hive that hummed in every cell
> Is now sealed honey-tight.
>
> His thought is tied, the curving prow
> Of motion moored to rock;
> And minutes burst upon a brow
> Insentient to shock.
>
> -Theodore Roethke, Death Piece[19]

In the medico-physiological definition of death,
the question of consciousness or awareness is only
obliquely considered, in that one of the criteria for
death is the irreversible cessation of spontaneous
cerebral functions. Now, however, death, considered
psychologically, is defined as the permanent loss of
consciousness, or perhaps more precisely, the loss of
embodied consciousness. Again, we are here avoiding
the question of any enduring non-bodily consciousness,
since that pertains to the state after death--if there
is one.[20]

The nature of death as the permanent loss of embodied consciousness leads inevitably to the quandry
which Freud raised: Is it possible for a human being
to imagine him/herself permanently "non-conscious"?
Or, more precisely without consciousness? Or are we so

"embodied" as it were in our consciousness that even
"outside" our bodies--if such a state is possible--we
are ineluctably tied to them, if only as spectators?
The subtle issue at stake here, of course, is the
meaning of consciousness. Obviously, if we define
death as the permanent cessation of consciousness,
then we assume that we know what it means to be conscious, as the following quote from Jorge Borges
suggests:

> The date which the chisel engraves in
> the tablet, and which is recorded in
> the parochial registers, is later than
> our own death; we are already dead when
> nothing touches us, neither a word nor
> a yearning nor a memory. I know that
> I am not dead.[21]

Some authors therefore have suggested that the psychological definition of death as the permanent cessation
of consciousness be modified to read "embodied" consciousness.[22] This provides a helpful clarification,
since we know what it is--at least experientially--to
be bodily conscious, that is our normal state of being-
human. Therefore it is not meaningless to say that
death is the cessation or loss of embodied consciousness.[23] We find ourselves operating here in the via
negativa of Thomas Aquinas and the scholastics regarding the transcendentals (God, beauty, truth, etc.):
we know more what they are not than what they are. It
seems perfectly legitimate in other words to define
death as the loss of embodied consciousness, since we
have a first-hand, experiential awareness of what it
means to be (bodily) conscious.[24] We have only speculation about "non-bodily" consciousness--if such is
even possible. In other words, the evidence for any
state of non-bodily consciousness (especially after-
death) would have no reliable scientific grounds.[25]

In sum, we may with good reason define death psychologically as the permanent loss of embodied human
consciousness. But this definition suggests an interesting correlation between the medico-physiological
and the psychological definitions of death, since in
fact the biological or physiological condition of the
cessation of cerebral functions results in the loss of
embodied human consciousness. Effectively, then,
through the physiological phenomenon of death, the "I,"
or "ego," or "self" which the individual person embodied ceases to be.[26] In this sense, the shift in

122

the medico-biological analysis of death from respiratory-circulatory functions to cerebral functions corresponds to the contemporary emphasis in psychology on human life as embodied human consciousness or awareness.

iii. PHILOSOPHICAL DEATH. It may very well be that we have already laid the groundwork for the conceptual analysis of death in our physiological and psychological reflections. The fact is that, assessing the meaning of death (that is, individual death) from the perspective of philosophy one would have to make some assumptions about the meaning of life, the concept of personal identity and the irrevocable fact of human and individual mortality and its effect on our general attitude toward all of reality.[27] In our discussion of the physiological and psychological definitions of death we have in effect already addressed the questions of the meaning of death and the concept of personal identity (personal center of consciousness). The third question regarding the brute fact of mortality and its impact on one's overall attitude to reality opens up two distinct issues: first, the concept of death as the stark realization of one's finitude; and, second, the effect of this realization on one's general orientation to reality. This latter issue leads directly into the question of one's response to death as limit-to life, but that is the topic of the next section on the limit-of death.

Therefore the central philosophical dimension which we have yet to attend to is the nature of death as the unmistakable signal of finitude and mortality. Most traditional philosophies, it seems fair to say, effectively avoided directly confronting this issue either because they followed a general Epicurean (or Neo-Epicurean) orientation, which asserts basically that while we are alive death is not, and after death we are not, so why worry about it.[28] Or else they concentrated on the second aspect of death and after-death, that is, personal survival. On the other hand, the contemporary philosophies of Existentialism and Phenomenology exhibit their own blind spot by concentrating on death as the annihilation of the ego. While hoping to avoid the excesses of such contemporary views, perhaps we can claim the same basic starting point, namely, the awareness of individual mortality, finitude, and cessation. The question is unambiguous: What happens to me? We are accustomed to use various diversionary tactics and harmless generalities to avoid

123

tackling this question. The traditional syllogism has the markings of such an evasion: all men are mortal; John is a man; therefore John is mortal. But the ultimate and timely application of that logic is not (just) to "John," but to oneself: "I will die," and What happens to me at death?"

The conundrum which philosophy faces in this question is that reflection can produce only "halting hypotheses and tentative constructs," and not "clear and incontrovertible truth."[29] I think the approach of Wittgenstein, and the philosophies of language generally offer meanings for death which are most directly related to the limit-to dimension under discussion here. "These meanings include 'the disappearance of the transcendental subject', 'the limit of the world', and 'the loss of a discourse'."[30] I would like here to concentrate specifically on Wittgenstein's interpretation of death as 'limit-to life'. There are two passages particularly which seem to focus Wittgenstein's views: "So too at death the world does not alter but comes to an end." And again, "Death is not an event in life: we do not live to experience death ... Our life has no end just as our visual field has no limit."[31] There is some discussion about the meaning of these texts as we noted earlier.[32] The general consensus, however, is that Wittgenstein is really applying his overall analysis of language to language about death. The key to understanding what Wittgenstein is saying is to link the preceding passages with the two principles from our earlier discussions. These are stated most clearly by Wittgenstein himself. First, his central aphorism from the Tractatus: "The limits of my language are the limits of my world,"[33] and the second principle, equally central in our study, "Man has the urge to thrust against the limits of language ... But the tendency, the thrust points to something..."[34] The first principle aptly paraphrases the notion of limit-to: with death the individual's world comes to an end; he no longer speaks a language (at least in any communicable way). This is a logical conclusion from his identification between language and world. This makes it possible for him to assert that death "is not an event in life. It is not a fact of the world."[35] Death is the 'limit' of my world, not in the sense of being part of that world, but rather that through it my world comes to an end. Thus "to speak of something beyond this limit as if my ordinary language could be used is not even to speak

important nonsense."[36] And so Wittgenstein denies the
possibility of saying anything at all (logically, or
even in the context of language games) about death.
This, however, does not mean that it may not point to
or show something. And this is precisely where the
second principle comes into play, that is, that the
urge to thrust against the limits to language points
to something. But that leads to our second chapter on
the limits-of death, that is, death as ground and
possibility.

To conclude this first chapter on death-as-limit-
to-life, that is, as finality, termination, end of
life, I would like to emphasize three points. First,
the demanding effort that is involved in imagining oneself dead, whether from a Freudian-Wittgensteinian
perspective (where the individual ceases to be), or
from the contemporary social perspective (where mortality is systematically avoided). Second, to come to
grips with death as limit-to human existence, we ap-
proached it from the viewpoints of biology, psychology
and philosophy. This exercise yielded some helpful
insights as well as a quite unified pattern for our
reflections. Biologically, death was described as the
permanent cessation of spontaneous cerebral functions.
This determination, we noted, has rather far-reaching,
pragmatic consequences, since it is used for organ
transplants. Taking a cue from medicine, we described
death psychologically as the permanent loss of embodied
consciousness. Freud notwithstanding, this definition
says--though negatively--something very powerful, since
everything--absolutely everything--that is included
under bodily consciousness, ceases to be. It is not
that we cannot imagine such a condition; it is rather
that we do not want to, and so we conveniently refuse.
Finally, from the vantage point of philosophy, death
was described basically in Wittgensteinian terms as
the limit-to life, where limit means both something
beyond experience and language, and at the same time
that which brings experience and language, that is,
world, to a close. Indeed, my world ends.

The third and concluding point to emphasize is
that there is a common narrative element surrounding
and pervading the physiological, psychological, and
philosophical definitions of death. This over-arching
narrative element is that the person, subject, "I,"
ceases to be entirely; my world comes to an end. I
think the simplest way to summarize this story is:

125

"I am and I shall die, but I do not know what to expect." Yevgeny Yevtushenko captures the image beautifully:

> In any man who dies there dies with him
> his first snow and kiss and fight.
>
> They are left books and bridges
> and painted canvas and machinery.
>
> Whose fate is to survive.
> But what has gone is also not nothing:
>
> by the rule of the game something has gone.
> Not people die but worlds die in them.[37]

Finally, Stewart Alsop, perhaps as frankly as imagination permits, expresses the sense of death as limit-to life:

> But the most important reason why I felt no
> panic fear last Saturday was, I think, the
> strange, unconscious, indescribable process
> which I have tried to describe in this book--
> the process of adjustment whereby one comes
> to terms with death. A dying man needs to
> die, as a sleepy man needs to sleep, and
> there comes a time when it is wrong, as well
> as useless, to resist...
> There is a time to live, but there is also
> a time to die. That time has not yet come
> for me. But it will. It will come for all
> of us.[38]

2. DEATH AS LIMIT-OF HUMAN EXISTENCE

> Where am I now? and what
> Am I to say portends?
> Death is but death, and not
> the most obtuse of ends.
>
> No matter how one leans
> One yet fears not to know.
> God knows what all this means!
> The mortal mind is slow.

Eternity is here
There is no other place.
The only thing I fear
Is the Almighty Face.

-Yvor Winters, <u>A Song in Passing</u>[39]

In the preceding chapter we focused attention on the dimension of death as limit-to life. Through the perspectives of medicine, psychology, and philosophy we accentuated the limits <u>to</u> death in order to <u>show</u> the limits <u>of</u> death. This is consistent with our continuing effort to link together the theology of limit and the theology of story. Since indeed theology of limit is related to theology of story as parable is related to myth, theology exercises a critically reflective function, checking and questioning the comprehensive and secure worlds that myth creates, and often absolutizes (that death, for example, is <u>merely</u> a transition). In fact, we have emphasized this function as centrally theological, since transcendence (or conversely, meaninglessness) emerges most surely at the moments of crisis and collapse of myths. At the same time, however, in the very exercise of its parabolic-reversal function, the theology of limit takes on dimensions of promise and possibility. Theology of limit joins forces with theology of story in the re-construction and re-presentation of human existence at the limits and edges--the limits and edges of death in this case. Paradox and parable therefore not only subvert and shatter existing and given worlds, but suggest in the very process alternative worlds.

In the previous chapter we saw in the experience of death a rather shattering and stark account of the limit-to life, the permanent cessation of embodied consciousness and the end of the person's world. In the face of the brute fact of mortality, of final human limitation, humans nonetheless manifest a strong tendency, to paraphrase Wittgenstein again, to push and strain at the limit that death is. But this urge, this thrust points to, or shows, something. To walk at the edges and limits is, as we have emphasized, to create the possibility of transcendence. Nonetheless, in the disclosure of this possibility and promise at the limits of life, one exercises wisely the same caution as in the other cases of pushing at the edges of language (sense? nonsense?) and at the limits of

127

environment (responsible intervention? or radical imbalance?).

The urge to thrust at the limit-to life that death is has resulted in three basic attitudes or stories about death as limitation. These are the stories of i) Systematic denial/avoidance/repression of death; ii) Acknowledgement of death as prelude to after-death; iii) Death as existential challenge to live. We will examine these stories individually.

i. DENIAL-AVOIDANCE-REPRESSION.

> Death is the least of things to be feared
> because while we are it is not
> and when it comes we are not
> and so we never meet it at all.
>
> That was a Greek way of avoiding the issue--
> which is, that ever since the blood-drenched
>   moment
> of primal recognition,
> death has lived all times in us
> and we in her, commingled,
> and not to recognize her is
> not to recognize ourselves.
>
> The lovely body is composed of what was dead
> and will be dead again. Death
> gives us birth, we live in her.
>
> -Frederick Morgan, Death Mother[40]

Frederick Morgan reminds us that the avoidance and repression of death is not only a contemporary American phenomenon, since Epicurus had already long ago formulated a rather tight philosophical position eliminating death as a significant human concern. Familiarity with Christian Scientists (surrounded by the dead and dying, and refusing to attend to those experiences) suggests another kind of denial of suffering and death. Finally, most other religious stories, too, although admitting the physical death of the individual, nonetheless emphasize so strongly something eternal and unchanging in the person (immortality of the soul, resurrection, reincarnation, etc.) that the brute fact of death and mortality is repressed. In a way, the stories relating to death over the centuries in most cultures have effectively attributed death to some "unfortunate accident that

128

took place in the beginning."[41] There has been a re-
curring conviction in cultural and religious stories
that humans are naturally immortal; natural death, in
other words, is unconceivable. Can we say then that
contemporary society in its avoidance-denial posture
is fully in the flow of history? I think the answer
is a qualified "no." What seems to characterize
modern attitudes, and what distinguishes these attitudes from traditional approaches are two important
factors. First, in traditional societies where death
was seen as unnatural there was nonetheless a creative
interpretation of death as complementary to life, as
the process whereby "new life" begins. It represents
a change in man's ontological status. Second, modern
society does not really have any first-hand experience
of death. There are death "experts," as it were, who
take care of all the functions that surround the event
of death. This has been referred to as the "institutionalization" of death, differing significantly from
the tribal and familial patterns of traditional
society. In our society institutions and professionals
are entrusted with the tasks of determining death, re-
moving the corpse, preparing it for "viewing," dis-
posing of it, and so forth. All of this has shielded
a large--if not the largest--segment of contemporary
society from that personal and interpersonal process
that dying must necessarily be.

These two factors, then, that is, the denial of
any positive function for death, and the virtually all-
pervasive institutionalization of death, have rendered
the current social-cultural phenomenon of avoidance
unique in cultural history.[42] Much has been written
about the contemporary attitudes toward death in
Western, and particularly American, culture.[43] It is
not my intention to review that literature here. There
are, however, some common themes spanning this recent
spate of literature on death. Three of these themes
help clarify the denial/avoidance posture of modern
society: a. Death as pornographic and forbidden; b.
Funeral practices relating to death; c. Problems of a
scientific-technological society: the medical model.

a. <u>Death as pornographic and forbidden</u>. This assessment of modern attitudes toward death is a paraphrase
of the classic study by Geoffrey Gorer, "The Pornography of Death,"[44] and the more recent historical
study of Philipe Aries, "Forbidden Death,"[45] and Aries
acknowledges his debt to Gorer. Following is Gorer's
own summary of his thesis:

> Traditionally, and in the lexicographic
> meaning of the term, pornography has been
> concerned with sexuality. For the greatest
> part of the last two hundred years copula-
> tion and (at least in the mid-Victorian
> decades) birth were the unmentionables of
> the triad of basic human experiences...
> During most of this period death was no
> mystery, except in the sense that death is
> always a mystery...
> In the twentieth century, however, there
> seems to have been an unremarked shift in
> prudery; whereas copulation has become more
> and more mentionable, particularly in Anglo-
> Saxon societies, death has become more and
> more "unmentionable" as a natural process.[46]

The pornography of death, then, follows the same
pattern as the Victorian prudishness toward sex.[47] And
just as the avoidance and repression of sex by the
Victorian society resulted in the sexual pornography
of contemporary society, so the contemporary repression and avoidance of death has resulted in a pornography of death. To put it another way, since death
cannot be represented naturally and normally, it is
spoken of and re-presented in all kinds of bizarre
ways, as exemplified in the mass media, which "make
little bid for our normal feelings of sorrow, guilt
and love at the occasion of death. The creators of
Mike Hammer and James Bond seemed only to be making
each successive novel contain more spectacular ways of
dying. And our response contains no more genuine human
feelings than that of the collection of filthy pictures.
So death not only surrounds us in our time, but we
search it out. We seek it in order to deny it."[48] In
a paradoxical sort of way Rudolph Otto's mysterium
tremens et fascinans seems to apply here. We are both
fascinated (in a kind of pornographic way) by death
and yet we tremble at its reality. Like a child in
the presence of a clown: on the one hand the child
wishes to approach the clown (fascination), but yet
instinctively shies away (trembling). This seems to
be our manner of dealing with death in contemporary
Western society. Since we cannot look directly at it
as a natural event in life, we find numerous bizarre
and impersonal ways to come at it obliquely. In the
words of one television executive in charge of
programming:

There's one constant in every successful
dramatic TV story form, and that's that
the leading character's occupation is
somehow connected with death. We've
tried stories about publicity men,
Congressmen, social workers. They've
all been unsuccessful. I don't know why,
but story forms connected with death are
the only ones that have audiences willing
to watch in numbers large enough to make
a dramatic series economically viable.[49]

b. <u>Funeral</u> <u>practices</u>.

I will teach you my townspeople
how to perform a funeral--
for you have it over a troop
of artists--
unless one should scour the world--
you have the ground sense necessary.

See the hearse leads.
I begin with a design for a hearse.
For Christ's sake not black--
nor white either--and not polished!
Let it be weathered--like a farm wagon--
with gilt wheels (this could be
applied fresh at small expense)
or no wheels at all:
a rough dray to drag over the ground.

Knock the glass out!
My God--glass, my townspeople!
For what purpose? Is it for the dead
to look out or for us to see
how well he is housed or to see
the flowers or the lack of them--
or what?
To keep the rain and snow from him?
He will have a heavier rain soon;
pebbles and dirt and what not.
Let there be no glass--
and no upholstery! phew!
and no little brass rollers
and small easy wheels on the bottom--
my townspeople what are you thinking of?

A rough plain hearse then
with gilt wheels and top it all
On this the coffin lies
by its own weight.

No wreaths please--
especially no hot-house flowers
Some common mememto is better
something he prized and is known by:
his old clothes--a few books perhaps--
God knows what! You realize
how we are about these things,
my townspeople--
something will be found--anything--
even flowers if he had come to that.
So much for the hearse.

For heaven's sake though see to the driver!
Take off the silk hat! In fact
there's no place at all for him
up there unceremoniously
dragging our friend out of his own dignity!
Bring him down--bring him down!
Low and inconspicuous! I'd not have him ride
on the wagon at all--damn him--
the undertaker's understrapper!
Let him hold the reins
and walk at the side
and inconspicuously too!

Then briefly as to yourselves:
Walk behind--as they do in France...
seventh class, or if you ride
Hell take curtains: Go with some show
of inconvenience; sit openly--
to the weather as to grief.
Or do you think you can shut grief in?
What--from us? We who have perhaps
nothing to lose? Share with us
share with us--it will be money
in your pockets.

                    Go now
I think you are ready.

                    -Carlos Williams, Tract$_{50}$

Carlos Williams' poem narrates both the conventional ritual of funeral practices and his criticism

of them. If our social and religious rituals do in fact manifest the values and beliefs of the society at any given time, then the funeral practices of twentieth-century North America are surely revealing. We have already alluded to the institutionalization of death as a significant factor in the general distancing of death in our society. This institutionalization is further aggravated by the standard American funeral practices. Though undoubtedly explainable historically and sociologically, these practices tell us much about our current posture of denial and avoidance. First of all, a semi-professional class has grown up to handle the business of "taking care of the dead," something traditionally attended to by family and friends. As a result the corpse is no longer laid out in the house, but in the funeral "parlor." Embalming and restorative cosmetics are practiced so that "viewing" or "visitation" may go on, almost as though the individual never died ("how nice he/she looks!"). "Comfort" caskets have replaced coffins, and thus the decor of the "slumber room" is unaffected.

While every society must have its rituals to attend to critical transitions in social interaction, the scenario of the "American Way of Death"[51] is one of deliberate avoidance of the reality of death and denial of the brute fact of mortality and corruption. Even if our funerary practices are the result of a complex mix of attitudes, motivations and values, they deserve close scrutiny, since in the final analysis they militate against any authentic awareness of death as limit-to life, that is, the termination in every experiential sense of personal bodily presence. Death as ground and possibility can only be truly understood if death is first seen starkly and unequivocally as finality and closure to life.

c. Death in a technological world: the medical model. Just as earlier in our discussion on the limits of environment, we isolated an attitude of domination on the part of contemporary technocratic man, so that same kind of attitude carries over directly to the experience of death. In the same way that the technocrat sees limits generally as obstacles and barriers to be eliminated, so the final limit-to human existence, death, becomes absolutely intolerable. Death confronts technocratic and scientific man with the ultimate phenomenon wherein "man experiences that in his very being there is a NOT, that he is not complete, that he has

133

<u>not</u> absolute control over his existence, that he is <u>not</u> sufficient to himself..."[52]

Perhaps the profession which most directly experiences this powerlessness--and its concomitant frustration--in the face of death is the medical profession. The classic response of the physician to the terminally ill patient is, "I can't do <u>anything</u> for you."[53] A sad confusion between curing and caring! This powerlessness of medical technology in such cases has dictated to a large extent professional attitudes of hospital staffs and related agencies to the terminally ill: isolation, pretense, avoidance, and so forth.[54] There is evident in this general posture an interesting tie-in between ecology-as-limit and death-as-limit and the response of a highly technocratic society: frustration and denial. The challenge is to learn "to live within (our) limits."

In concluding our analysis of the first story or response to the limits-to death, we note that there is a massive reluctance within a large segment of the society to admit death in any authentic fashion. The tendency of this approach is to shy away from the reality of death in every imaginable way: not to speak about it (e.g., the common euphemisms, "pass away," "pass on," "meet one's maker"), not to encounter it in the world of corpses (institutionalization), and finally not to be with the dying--at least not to let on (avoidance) that there is such a state as "dying." And <u>then</u> we die; then is <u>not</u> <u>now</u>; and that's that![55]

ii. DEATH AS PRELUDE TO AFTER-DEATH. This second story of personal encounter with the limit-to death reflects on the one hand a frank affirmation of the reality of death, but then in virtually the same breath begins conversation about after-death existence. This conversation may be based on philosophical speculation about the immortality of the soul; it may result from religious belief in resurrection, reincarnation, or some similar eternal existence in a more or less modified human form; it may be based finally on parapsychological findings relating to altered states of consciousness. Whatever the basis for belief in after-death experiences, one runs the obvious risk of diverting attention away from the primary--ontologically and chronologically--reality of death as limitation, end, termination.

It may well be that the stories of something
eternal and unchanging which guarantees eternal existence are simply rationalizations deriving from the
inability of humans to imagine their own death, since
"in the unconscious every one of us is convinced of
his own immortality."[56] Or it may be in fact that the
human person is not able readily to divide death and
after-death for purposes of reflection, meditation and
study. The question, in other words, is whether it is
possible to think about death--except perhaps in the
rarified atmosphere of philosophical speculation--
without at the same time and necessarily imagining some
kind of survival. Not only is this Freud's conviction
it is attested to also by the fact that there is no
religious tradition--at least among the major world
religions--which does not have some kind of story
about life after death.[57] Perhaps the issue here for
the theology of limit is not whether stories about life
after-death--or the survival hypothesis--are meaningful, but rather whether the emphasis on after-death
experiences detracts from the confrontation with death
as limit-to life. For sure, in narratives which assume
afterlife, the limit-of dimension of death is readily
apparent, that is, death as ground, possibility and
disclosive of a further (fuller?) reality. Consistent
with the principles of the theology of limit, however,
we emphasize the limit-to life in order to show the
limit-of life. And so both dimensions of death are
essential. The only question is whether limit-of life,
the second aspect of death, necessarily includes personal survival in some new and altered state of consciousness.[58] And that takes us to the third story
regarding death as limit-of life.

iii. DEATH AS EXISTENTIAL CHALLENGE TO LIVE.

> The confrontation with death--and the
> reprieve from it--makes everything look
> so precious, so sacred, so beautiful
> that I feel more strongly than ever
> the impulse to love it, to embrace it,
> and to let myself be overwhelmed by it.
> My river has never looked so beautiful
> ... Death, and its ever present possi-
> bility, makes love, passionate love,
> more possible. I wonder if we could
> love passionately, if ecstasy would be
> possible at all, if we knew we'd never
> die.
> —Abraham Maslow[59]

It is difficult to mask one's preferred story
about reality; and this is the case with this third
narrative about death as limit-of human existence. We
have seen two stories so far describing ways in which
humans cope with the limits-to life that death presents. These are, first, the story of avoidance and
denial, which is to live really as though death were
not part of the human scenario; and, secondly, the
story of afterlife, that is, some form of survival in
an unending state of personal awareness. This again,
though obviously not an overt mechanism for denial,
more often than not produces the same general effect.

     The third account about death as the limit-of
life is one particularly characteristic of the
twentieth century and its existentialist and linguistic philosophical orientation. The following com-
mentaries on Heidegger and Wittgenstein are helpful
introductions to this mentality:

>   Death is that ultimate phenomenon whereby
> man experiences that in his very being
> there is a NOT, that he is not complete,
> that he has not absolute control over his
> existence, that he is not sufficient to
> himself. For every human being, death
> is an end and limits one's potentiality as
> a whole. But death, Heidegger maintains,
> is not only a biological limit ("Being-at-
> an-end"). First and foremost it is an
> ontological limit ("Being-toward-an-end"),
> and one which is experienced uniquely and
> individually by each human being. In con-
> fronting death, man confronts his end and
> experiences finitude, that there is an un-
> fathonable element to his existence over
> which he has no control, that there is a
> "not yet" in his being which can never be
> overcome... If he can accept Death as an
> ungetoverable aspect of his being, he ac-
> cepts the whole of his being, lets himself
> into the "dual realm" (the unity in dif-
> ference of being) and acknowledges the es-
> sential mystery in his existence--that in
> the last analysis he cannot be a creature
> of indomitable control. This frees him
> from the domination of particular ends for
> his whole potentiality...[60]

Heidegger's distinction between death as both a biological limit and an ontological limit closely parallels the distinction we have been making between death
as limit-to life and death as limit-of life respec-
tively. In a somewhat similar bein, William Breuning
analyzes Wittgenstein's views on death as limit:

> Death-talk is of paramount importance to
> Wittgenstein and can be used as a crucial
> experiment for the validity of his philo-
> sophical views. He consistently denies
> the possibility of <u>saying</u> at the level of
> depth grammar <u>anything</u> at all about death...
> But this does <u>not mean</u> that it <u>cannot show</u>
> <u>anything</u>. Whether it shows anything or
> not, that is, whether it is important or
> unimportant nonsense, depends on what the
> speaker takes the talk to be about, on what
> picture he has, on what games he takes him-
> self to be playing. If he takes himself to
> be playing games of <u>transcendent language</u>,
> then he <u>neither</u> says <u>anything</u> <u>nor</u> <u>shows any-</u>
> <u>thing</u>. If, on the other hand, he speaks a
> <u>transcendental</u> <u>language</u>, a language about
> the limits of language, then, although he
> <u>cannot say</u> anything, he <u>can</u> <u>show</u> something.
> And what he shows concerns the existential
> character of his own life. It shows his
> fears or his happiness, his basic harmony
> with the world or his disharmony. It shows
> if he exists as a human being or not.[61]

In the existential character of death, then, we find a
story that combines in healthy tension the two elements
that seem to be problematic in the other two stories.
The story of denial and avoidance clearly does not deal
with the reality of death in any authentic fashion.
Life is lived in spite of death instead of towards
death. In the accounts involving life after death,
death is certainly incorporated into the narrative, but
it does not somehow stand clearly before us as the
absolute end of existence as we know it. One cannot
help but think of Rainer Maria Rilke's linking of
poetry and death, especially as symbolized by the
mythical poet Orpheus for whom death became the occasion for song:

Only one who has lifted the lyre
Among shadows too,
May divining render
The infinite praise.

Only who with the head has eaten
Of the poppy that is theirs,
Will never again lose
The most delicate tone.

Though the reflection in the pool
Often swims before one's eyes
Know the image.

Only in the dual realm
Do voices become
Eternal and mild.

Sonnets to Orpheus[62]

The existential encounter with death, therefore,
combines in one story the reality of death as limit-to
life, as the complete end and total termination of my
life as I know it (not necessarily affirming or
denying any other consciousness that succeeds this
embodied consciousness), and also limit-of life, that
is, the ground, starting-point, possibility and
promise for authentic human existence. One does not
begin to live ("authentically," in Heideggerian terms)
until one faces the reality of death. Death, as it
were, calls attention to the quality of one's life, as
Maslow's reflections so eloquently show. Existence is
graciously given, and can cease at any time; one
comes, therefore, to treasure the present (containing
the past and looking toward the future). Such seem to
be the thoughts of the historian Cornelius Ryan, re-
corded while terminally ill:

Each morning for the past two or three
years when I have awakened the first
words I've said are, 'Thank you, God,
for this fine day.' It has not mattered
if the weather was bad or good. What
has been important is that God has seen
me through the night and given me another
day to work and to be with my family...
I have received more than my share of
blessings. I have been able to cram so
much into my life that it has been brimful

of happiness. The most rewarding
moments ... all have been realized
in the years since I have had cancer.[63]

Finally, any description of death as the existential challenge to live would be seriously deficient
if it did not acknowledge that there are dimensions of
the existentialist narrative which lead to excesses in
the opposite direction. Concretely, death as the
limit-of existence effectively disintegrates in some
existentialist and phenomenological modes of thought,
since in their emphasis as absolute end, and, fixing
simultaneously on many of the absurdities of human
existence, they find life itself not worth living. In
this perspective (represented especially by Sartre and
Beckett) looking into the stark reality of death leads
to nothingness, to the unshakable conviction that the
human enterprise itself is absurd. It is impossible
existentially to prove that it's worth committing oneself to the human "project" (to God?). And perhaps
this is the mystery of faith and the power of parable.
One does not know what follows death--if indeed any-
thing--, and yet one finds this very experience of
void and nothingness--as possibility--liberating.
Some of Ernest Becker's reflections express rather
directly this paradox:

> What makes dying easier is to be able
> to transcend the world in some kind of
> religious dimension (not necessarily in
> personal mortality or anything like
> that). I would say that the most im-
> portant thing is to know that beyond
> the absurdity of one's life, beyond the
> human viewpoint, beyond what is
> happening to us, there is the fact of
> the tremendous creative energies of the
> cosmos that are using us for some pur-
> pose we don't know. To be used for
> divine purposes, however we may be mis-
> used, this is the thing that consoles...
> I think one does, or should try to, just
> hand over one's life, the meaning of it,
> the value of it, the end of it. This
> has been the most important to me. I
> think it is very hard for secular man
> to die.[64]

It is possible, therefore, to imagine two responses to

the existential challenge of death. The affirmative attitude acknowledges the sense of death as the limit-of life, that is, as ground and possibility. In the words of Colleen Clements, "for those of us, however, who have maintained, no matter how difficult or qualified, an affirmative attitude toward reality, all human activites and undertakings are still possible. The countless problems and games of the universe remain options for us."[65] T. S. Eliot captures this modified optimism, I think:

> I said to my soul, be still, and wait
>   without hope
> For hope would be hope for the wrong
>   thing; wait without love
> For love would be love of the wrong
>   thing; there is yet faith
> But the faith and love and the hope are
>   all in the waiting.
> Wait without thought, for you are not
>   ready for thought:
> So the darkness shall be the light, and
>   the stillness the dancing.
>
> —Four Quartets: East Coker.[66]

The negative attitude on the contrary cannot really get beyond the fact of death as limitation, end, finality. "His (negativist) logical conclusion, his logical act is negation, and that implies termination of existence. No dialogue is possible here. We merely request the nay-sayer to act upon his conviction and negate existence, and one cannot discourse with nothing."[67]

To summarize this chapter, then, we have examined three stories regarding the limits-of death, that is, how humans might respond to death as limit-to life. The first account is the story of denial and avoidance. It is to act as though there were no such reality as death, knowing all the while of course that it is there, but acting as though one were immortal. As Ernest Becker notes:

> We build character and culture in order
> to shield ourselves from the devastating
> awareness of our underlying helplessness
> and the terror of our inevitable death...
> ... All humanly caused evil is based

> on man's attempt to deny his creature-
> liness, to overcome his insignificance.
> All the missiles, all the bombs, all
> human edifices, are attempts to defy
> eternity by proclaiming that one is not
> a creature, that one is something special...
> 68

The second response to the limit-to dimension of death
is the common narrative--whatever its particular di-
rection--of life after death. As we emphasized, this
story begins with a more or less firm statement about
death as the end of this life (death-resurrection),
but ineluctably connected with this affirmation is the
more or less elaborate story (for example, separation
of body and soul, "flight" of soul to the judgment
seat of God, final sentence, heaven (purgatory)or
hell) of an eternal existence in some form or other
in another place. As universal and religiously
soothing (or philosophically satisfying) as these
stories may be, yet at the one time when death is most
obvious, religion flees into truths of eternal life,
or philosophy advances proofs of immortality. That
little item in between life and eternity--as they have
it--gets lost, that is, death.69

The third--and preferred--response to death as
limit-to life is the story about death as existential
challenge to live authentically. It re-presents (re-
mythicizes) death as opening up to us (or opening us
up to) the authentic possibilities of human existence.
Although the existential approach to death does not
address the question of survival after death, it nonetheless incorporates creatively both the limit-to
dimension of death (human finitude and mortality) and
the limit-of death (ground and possibility). Perhaps
our rather folksy mode of conveying this reality is
through the paradox that the meaning of life is found
in the meaning of death. Further, the existentialist
position need not raise the question of life after
death, since death as the ontological context of life
addresses one existentially about the quality and
meaning of one's life. Authenticity derives from the
inherent worthwhileness of what one is doing--not from
some future reward or punishment which one might
receive.

As footnote to this chapter, I think Lawrence
Kohlberg's stages of moral development may have some

bearing on the stories of afterlife as being primarily
reward and punishment. This is the stage of childhood.
Adults act not for reward and punishment, but out of
conviction--at least ideally (the highest level of
moral development).

3.   RELIGIOUS STORIES AND DEATH

> Life, it seems, is this;
> To learn to shorten what has moved amiss;
> To temper motion till a mean is hit,
> Though the wild meaning would unbalance it;
> To stand, precarious, near the utter end;
> Betrayed, deserted, and alone descend,
> Blackness before, and on the road above
> The crowded terror that is human love;
> To still the spirit till the flesh may lock
> Its final cession in eternal rock.
>
> Then let me pause in this symbolic air,
> Each fiery grain immobile as despair,
> Fixed at a rigid distance from the earth,
> Absorbed each motion that arose from birth.
> Here let me contemplate eternal peace,
> Eternal station, which annuls release.
> Here may I read its meaning, though the eye
> Sear with effort, ere the body die.
> For what one is, one sees not; 'tis the lot
> Of him at peace to contemplate it not.
>
> -Yvor Winters, The Grave[70]

We have been exploring the reality of death and
the experience of limits so far in this part of our
essay. Our methodology has been centered on the theology of limit. Accordingly, we discussed death both
as the limit-to life, that is limitation and threat,
and death as the limit-of life, that is existential
challenge to (an) integral and authentic human existence. In this third chapter we will be looking at
the issue of religious language and story, that is,
the language and story adequate to the limit-situations
and limit-questions encountered in the human experience
of dying and death. The Tao Teh Ching, a most popular
scripture of Taoism, contains a kind of summary of
virtually all religious stories about death:

One who becomes aware of his permanence/is
    wise
Wise/he is just
Just/he is serene.
Serene/he is of a heavenly nature.
Of a heavenly nature/he is united with Tao.
United with Tao/he is eternal.
Thus the circle closes.
Sure of the eternity of his Self/
the loss of his body leaves him serene.[71]

Central to all religions is the story--more or
less elaborate, depending on the religion--of some
kind of existence after death.[72] As Mircea Eliade
points out: "in archaic societies ideas of human
perenniality can still be detected, that is, the conviction that human beings, though no longer immortal,
could live indefinitely if only a hostile agent did
not put an end to their lives. In other words, a
natural death is inconceivable..."[73] And later in the
same context, "We are assured of one fact: everywhere
in the traditional world death is, or was, considered
a second birth, the beginning of a new spiritual
existence."[74]

This general thrust of all religions to develop
some kind of story about the "other" world and the
process (general funerary rituals[75]) which initiate
one into the new life, also represents something of a
problem in view of the theology of limit. Concretely,
the issue is whether the traditional religious
stories--necessary as they are[76]--gloss over the stark
reality of death. John Dominic Crossan raises the
question in bold terms:

> I have tried to raise three consecutive and
> connected questions which seem to me
> crucial for the future of Christian faith.
> In their unity they ask whether immortality,
> however carefully couched in terms of divine
> gift, is an intrinsically idolatrous refusal
> to accept our destined mortality and our
> inevitable finitude... We shall have to
> start looking with calm eyes into the harsh
> darkness of our own finitude and to begin
> in such asceticism to prepare for an ex-
> perience of God and of Christ that may
> speak to our exhausted spirituality with a

force strong enough to infuse our modernity
with a renewed faith and not just with what
has become for us now a repeated
superstition...[77]

In an equally direct indictment Robert Neale, commenting on the mediating role of clergymen in the experience of death, writes: "At the one time when
death is most obvious to a Christian community the
Church flees into dogmas of eternal life..."[78] Now,
in discussing death in our religious stories, I shall
address the question specifically of death as limit-to
life, and more precisely in relation to what these
stories say, in their more or less elaborate accounts,
about what follows death. Finally, I will limit any
extended comments to the Christian tradition of death
and resurrection, following this with some general
reflections on other religious stories about after-
death existence and experience.

i. CHRISTIAN STORY OF DEATH AND BODILY RESURRECTION.

What if it should turn out eternity
Was but the steeple on our house of life
That made our house of life a house of
    worship?
We do not go up there to sleep at night.
We do not go up there to live by day.
Nor need we ever go up there to live.
A spire and belfry coming on the roof
Means that a soul is coming on the flesh.

-Robert Frost, A Steeple on the House[79]

Even though the terse article from the Creed, "I
believe in the resurrection of the dead (and life
everlasting)" has been an integral element in
Christian belief from the very beginning, yet a more
ready response from Christians for many centuries to
the question about man's lot after death has been, "I
believe in the immortality of the soul." This development proved ultimately problematic, since it re-
presented a shift away from a generalized belief in
personal survival (import of "bodily resurrection") to
a belief in a purely spiritual reality. The next step
was to construct "another world" (the "real" world)
around the separated soul or spirit: thus the doctrines of purgatory, heaven (Beatific Vision = the
essence of Beatitude, a purely spiritual experience),

and hell (separation of soul from God and resulting punishment). In effect, then, the resurrection of the body had nothing to do ultimately with blessedness and damnation. This bizarre development in Christian eschatology led eventually to the rejection of matter and material reality, and finally the world itself. The real world was the world of the spirit (spirituality, life of the spirit, salvation of one's soul, and so forth).

This development led to several unfortunate conclusions. First, death was not seen as the real dissolution of the person, since the soul was the essential element in the composite.[80] The separation of the soul from the body 'freed' the soul for its true and proper modus existendi, that is, as a pure spirit. Second, Christians have tended to look merely to the future, to the things of the "next world," counting the things of earth as nothing, as mere shadows of the true realities (Neo-platonic influence) to come, and valueless when the perfect heavenly things shall have arrived.[81] The vision finally of the destruction of this world (fiery judgment) has led Christians to reject it as far as possible (religious life, anchorites, and so forth), and where not possible, to resign themselves to it in a spirit of renunciation, penance, and mortification.[82] Several points need to be made about the Christian story. First, it seems obvious that the story of bodily resurrection is in itself quite consistent with the general orientation of all religions to support some kind of after-life-- almost as a condition of their own validity. Religion is expected to respond to the central (depth) human mysteries. Certainly death (as well as the mysteries of origins and the mystery of suffering and evil) is such a depth dimension. One might, in fact, marvel at the simplicity of the Christian Creed: "I believe in the resurrection of the dead (body, flesh) and life everlasting." This tenet satisfied one of the primary elements of the classic comprehensive myths, namely, the coincidentia oppositorum. In this case the opposition is encountered in the belief on the one hand in a spiritual element in man, and at the same time the obvious total corruption of the body. The myth gains immeasurably in significance of course when it is linked to the death-resurrection of Jesus the Christ. The early and vague hints and progressive Old Testament belief in the resurrection of the body reached unique and consummate fulfillment in the death-

resurrection of Jesus. One almost feels about death
in such a story what Walt Whitman wrote in The Carol
of Death:

> Come lovely and soothing death
> Undulate round the world, serenely arriving,
>   arriving,
> In the day, in the night, to all, to each,
> Sooner or later delicate death.
>
> Praised be the fathomless universe,
> For life and joy, and for object and know-
>   ledge curious,
> And for love, sweet love--but praise! praise!
>   praise!
> For the sure-enwinding arms of cool-enfolded
>   death.[83]

But, as the theme of resurrection gradually grew
into the truth of immortality of the soul, the imagination, which was challenged in a creative way with
"resurrection," was progressively stifled with ready-
made philosophical answers to the depth questions
surrounding dying and death. What is death? Death is
the separation of body and soul.[84] What happens to
the soul? The soul, as the substantial element in the
composite, continues to exist and moves on to the
judgment "seat" of God, where it is the subject of
particular judgment. What happens to the body? It
returns to the earth from which it came. What happens
to the person? The soul is essentially the person,
and the soul retains a transcendental relationship to
the body until the time of General Resurrection when
the body and soul are "gloriously" rejoined.

What was the end result of this transition in
Christian tradition from resurrection to immortality
of the soul? First of all, there was a gradual
diminution of the event of death and a progressive
emphasis on the events after death. This was followed
by the gradual emergence of those events and the future
life as the dominant theme in religious eschatological
thinking and worship. The end term of the whole process was the effective denial of death (in its existential reality) in favor of the glory of afterlife.
One sees a clear expression of this transition in
James Weldon Johnson's poem Go Down Death:

146

Weep not, weep not
She is not dead;
She's resting in the bosom of Jesus.
Heart-broken husband -- weep no more;
Grief-stricken son -- weep no more;
Left-lonesome daughter -- weep no more;
She's only gone home...[85]

The direction of the Christian story, therefore, led
inevitably away from the notion of death as the absolute and dramatic end of the person (embodied consciousness), that is, away from death as limit-to
life and toward death primarily as transition, re-
lease, and passage. In sum, death as limit-to life
was effectively undermined in the emphasis on death
as limit-of human existence. Death _and_ resurrection
gave way ultimately to death _for_ immortality. That
is indeed a different story![86]

ii. OTHER RELIGIOUS STORIES. First of all, there is
a general consensus among historians of religions that
all of the major world religions share some form of
belief in personal survival, from resurrection to reincarnation.[87] These different religions may place
more or less emphasis on the individual identity of
the surviving subject (anatta of Buddhism's _nirvana_);
they may have a more or less central place for the
deity in the death-event (for example, immediate judgment in Christianity--Roman Catholicism particularly--
and natural processes in Chinese religions); finally,
these religions may vary in their perception of afterlife as the continuity of this life (earliest conception of religions, e.g., mummification and victuals
for the "journey"), or as the radical transformation
in another life (spiritual existence in a spiritual
world). Despite this radical pluralism among the
world religions (and indeed even in pre-literate
societies), they all gave a central role to the notion
and myths of afterlife.[88]

To make any comprehensive, abstract statement
about whether belief in an afterlife in the major
world religions deterred the religious followers in
these societies from authentically confronting the
reality of death is risky at best. I think perhaps
the story told about Chuang Tzu best characterizes the
traditional religious submission before the reality
of death:

Chuang Tzu's wife died. When Hui Tzu went
to convey his condolences, he found Chuang
Tzu sitting with his legs sprawled out,
pounding in a tub and singing. "You lived
with her, she brought up your children and
grew old," said Hui Tzu. "It should be
enough simply not to weep at her death.
But pounding on a tub and singing--this is
going too far, isn't it?" Chuang Tzu said,
"You're wrong. When she first died, do you
think I didn't grieve like anyone else?
But I looked back to her beginning and the
time before she was born. Not only the
time before she was born, but the time before she had a body. Not only the time before she had a body, but the time before
she had a spirit. In the midst of the
jumble of wonder and mystery a change took
place and she had a spirit. Another change
and she had a body. Another change and she
was born. Now there's been another change
and she's dead. It's just like the progression of the four seasons, spring, summer,
fall and winter.

Now she's going to lie down peacefully in
a vast room. If I were to follow after her
bawling and sobbing, it would show that I
don't understand anything about fate. So I
stopped. 89

The religious stories about afterlife rather than
shielding their adherents from the stark reality of
death provided them with a framework within which to
integrate death into the living process.

One may very well conclude from the perspective
of a twentieth century existentialist-phenomenologist
that such myths, rather than hold together in creative
tension the polar opposites of corruption of the
"flesh" and the experience of spirit, instead destroyed
one element of the polarity, namely, the reality of
death. At the same time, what we do not always see in
retrospect is that all cultures did in fact experience
directly the reality of death. They did not have
"professionals" to handle the true familial and tribal
tasks of preparing the corpse for burial, digging the
grave (preparing the funeral pyre, or whatever), and
overseeing the funerary rituals generally. Such

natural, first-hand experiences throughout life would have made it very difficult for them not to have faced directly and squarely the stark reality of death. Furthermore, tied to the land as they were, the natural rhythms of nature, as Chuang Tzu suggests, would be to them a constant reminder of the life cycles, from which clearly man was not exempt. This undoubtedly was the practical context within which the religious myths of afterlife originated and developed.[90]

The possibility of glossing over the fact of death in view of the promise of a "new" life is surely there in religious myths of afterlife. That the various cultures did in fact do so is certainly a debatable question. The myths and rituals surrounding death in the religions of the world furnish the richest examples of reconciling those apparent opposites of indestructible consciousness or spirit and corruptible flesh. Emily Dickinson appears to have captured the mythical power:

> The world is not conclusion;
>   A sequel stands beyond,
> Invisible, as music,
>   But positive, as sound.
> It beckons and it baffles;
>   Philosophies don't know
> And through a riddle, at the last;
>   Sagacity must go.
> To guess it puzzles scholars;
>   To gain it, men have shown
> Contempt of generations,
>   And crucifixion know.

-Bulletins from Immortality[91]

Any conclusion to these reflections on death and afterlife in religious traditions would need to be drawn in the full awareness of our theology of limit. The stories ideally would emphasize death as the limit-to life unequivocally, while simultaneously supplementing, or complementing, that limitation with whatever further reality that event foreshadowed, pointed to, initiated, or finalized. I find that the two contrasting statements of Albert Camus and Mircea Eliade frame the issue concisely. Camus writes: "If there is a sin against life perhaps it is not so much in giving up hope in it as it is to hope for another life and to rob oneself of the implacable grandeur of this life."[92] Eliade suggests the opposite: "Death is inconceivable if it is not related to a new form of being in some way or other, no matter how this form may be imagined."[93] This contrast sets the context for our next area of concern.

iii. RE-TELLING THE STORY.

> Though you may find me picking flowers
> Or washing my body in a river, or kicking
>   rocks,
> Don't think my eyes don't hold yours.
> And look hard upon them
> and drop tears as long as you stay before me
> Because I live as a man who knows death
> and I speak the only truth
> to those who will listen.
>
> Never yield a minute to despair, sloth,
>   fantasy.
> I say to you, you will face pain in your life
> You may lose your limbs, bleed to death
> Shriek for hours on into weeks in unimagin-
>   able agony.
> It is not aimed at anyone
> but it will come your way.
> The wind sweeps over everyone.
>
> You must bare your heart and expect nothing
>   in return.
> You must respond totally to nature.
> You must return to your simple self.
> I do not fool you. There lies no other path.
> I have not forsaken you, but I cannot be
>   among you all.
> You are not alone
> so long as you love your own true simple
>   selves.
> Your natural hair, your skin, your graceful
>   bodies,
> your knowing eyes and your tears and tongues.
>
> I stand before you all aching with truth
> Trembling with desire to make you know.
> Eat, sleep, and be serious about life.
> To be serious is to be simple;
> to be simple is to love....

-Ted Rosenthal, How Could I Not Be Among You?[94]

150

Ted Rosenthal represents a particularly interesting phenomenon of our generation: terminally ill
persons who share their last years, days, and even
moments with a wide public as well as with their own
immediate family and kin. This phenomenon in turn is
gradually challenging the public to look realistically
at the fact of dying and death. This broad sharing of
the experience of dying and anticipation of death is
parabolic in a real sense in contemporary society,
since it represents a reversal of the recent tradition
and expectations of denial, avoidance, and repression.
It is a radically new way of telling the story!

In our earlier reflections we delineated one of
the functions of the theology of limit as the re-
telling and re-presenting of the classic, traditional
story. We noted at that time also that within the
parabolic, paradoxical modes of story (particularly,
in the case at hand, the existentialist challenge of
death), that is, the limit-to death, we began already
to see the possibilities of re-constructing and remythicizing. More directly to the point, I isolated
two particular skills necessary to the delicate craft
of re-presenting and re-constructing, in this case,
the story of death as limit-of human existence. These
are, first, an understanding of the rhetoric of narrative, to repeat Brian Wicker's terminology, that is,
the rhetoric not only of the originating--or
normative--stories, but also of current fiction. The
second skill entails grasping the metaphysics of
belief. Again this is Brian Wicker's terminology, and
he understands by metaphysics of belief the philosophical (and/or doctrinal) assumptions of the community
creating and handing on the stories.[95]

a. Rhetoric of narrative. We are referring essentially to the process of communication which goes on
between the author and the reader. If we apply this
concept to the eschatological themes in the biblical
narratives, we might reasonably settle on the following interpretation. The two words that most accurately
portray the overall biblical story (myth with its
historical orientation) are promise and kingdom. The
Jews and successively the Christians are a people of
promise and the promise is that of final restoration
and exaltation, the Kingdom (of God). The historic-
linear conception of time is uniquely biblical, and
the future is thus always the time of promise. One is
continually struck by the emphasis on the "people" as

well as—if not more than—the individual. Communal
eschatology is at least as important as personal
survival.[96]   To repeat, the Old Testament story is
characterized by the historical nature of its
thought.[97]   It is structured concretely around the
history of a people; the interpretation of their
history becomes paradigmatic for all history.   The
central historical event is described (symbolized) in
the promises of Yahweh to Abraham (our father).   The
remainder of the story effectively winds around the
interpretation, retraction, and renewal of these
promises.   More broadly, it is in their history that
Yahweh is working out his master-plan for humankind.[98]

The transition from Old Testament theology of
promise and the restoration of the (chosen) people
(nation) to the New Testament notion of personal resurrection and Kingdom theology represents indeed a
significant shift in the direction of the story.
From that point on the story develops in at least two
different directions.   The reason apparently for this
divergence is the emergence of the theory of (bodily)
resurrection.   Without tracing in detail the development of semitic thought on the resurrection of the
dead, we need to highlight some pivotal moments in
this development.   Certain it is that by the end of
the Old Testament period belief in the resurrection of
the dead was a definite option in the religious story.
This development seems to be rooted in the miraculous
restoration of certain people to life by Elias and
Elisha (3 and 4 Kings).   Even though there the concern
is with restoration to the conditions of earthly existence (as is the case also with Lazarus in John,
II), yet one finds these incidents representing a type
or exemplar of the restoration (exaltation) of the
(chosen) people.   In due time Ezekiel's vision of the
dry bones becomes in a special way the symbol of
Israel's restoration (resurrection and exaltation).
Whatever the progressive development of this belief,
it is certain that with Daniel (12, 2-3) the resurrection connected now also with the apocalyptic movement is part of the biblical heritage.   The continua-
tion of this theme through 2 Machabees (Ch. 7) leads
one to the conclusion that at the time of Jesus the
idea of resurrection (linked to belief in the restoration of Israel) was well ingrained in Jewish
thought.[99]   It was not, however, universally accepted.
This fact is evident from Jesus' dispute with the
Sadducees, who did not accept resurrection philosophy.

The New Testament and early Christian accounts
of death-resurrection represents a complex development from the Jewish notion of promise and inheri-
tance to the New Testament "proclamation" by Jesus
of the "Kingdom of God," a notion still initially
shot through with temporal and political overtones.
As Norman Perrin points out:

> There is no doubt that the proclamation
> of the Kingdom of God is the central
> aspect of the message of Jesus. But
> having said that, one has to ask what
> it means to say that Jesus proclaimed
> the Kingdom of God. "Kingdom of God"
> is an apocalyptic symbol, a way of
> talking about God's final redemption
> of the world and of his people in the
> world; it is a form of the apocalyptic
> hope. To use the expression "Kingdom
> of God" is to speak of God acting as
> King, to speak of him visiting and
> redeeming his people, and this is the
> central theme of the message of Jesus.[100]

In time, however, Jesus progressively subverted all
notions of "kingdom" as political, temporal, or even
geographical, reducing (or expanding?) it to mean the
shattering of all human certainty about all final
realities. Jesus himself thus becomes the parable,
as it were, as well as the teller of parables pro-
claiming the Kingdom. Crossan deftly summarizes
Jesus' parabolic existence:

> ...There was the Cross, and the immediate
> conclusion was that it represented the
> divine rejection of Jesus. But if Jesus'
> parabolic vision was correct, then the
> Cross itself was not rejection but was
> itself the great Parable of God... Jesus
> died as parabler and rose as Parable.[101]

Jesus' story then is fundamentally and primarily
parable; it is the deliberate and continual subversion
of all master-stories about reality, including (and
maybe especially) the Old Testament promise and historical restoration story (myth) and the New Testament
political kingdom myth. Death-resurrection, the New
Testament paradigm, does not refer primarily, there-

fore, to the physical reality of dying and living on in some other place (or state), or even the restoration of this place; it refers rather to the fact that all our projects, all of our plans, and all blueprints for the predictable future are relative. They are our stories, our creations. Death as the ultimate parable or paradox is the symbol of the relativity of all our projects, since with death our world (story-reality) comes to an end. What death is beyond that--if anything--is mystery.

All the while, however, death as a future certainty checks and challenges us continually on the quality (Heidegger's "authenticity") of our lives. What do I take to be real, significant, valuable, worthwhile in view of the ultimate cessation of everything "I" know? Death is the one certain experience over which I have no ultimate control. Resurrection means affirmation in the face of the ultimate mystery of life--death. It may be that there is personal survival after death, but the complete, comfortable superstructure, woven out of the mythical tendencies to remove contradiction and reduce terror, must be seen precisely as such. The courageous, authentic and religious act is to affirm existence, life and possibility in the face of death, mortality and finitude. That, it seems to me, is the substance of the Christian story.

b. Metaphysics of belief. The question at issue here is: What precisely were the assumptions underlying the traditional story about death and resurrection? It is a very taxing question, not only in itself but also because of the vast overlay of cultural and philosophical accretions during the centuries spanning the New Testament era and the nascent Christian community. The foundational assumption of the Christian story about eschatology, it seems fair to say, is the death-resurredtion dyad (the death-resurrection event of Christ focusing the originating story). There are again two further assertions imbedded in that primary assumption. First, death is the end of all activity for the individual, being the total break-up of the person. Second, resurrection, as a kind of counterpoint, asserts that death is not the absolute end. It seems to require that the person live forever, but without any specific delineation of the conditions of that existence ("I believe in the resurrection of the dead and life everlasting").[102]

154

The philosophical, theological, and doctrinal additions that grew up around these two simple and elegant statements of belief are all later developments intended to flesh out in one way or another the raw-boned narrative elements in the nascent Christian community's story. The two primary instances of such later, explanatory additions are: first, death as the separation of body and soul, and, second, resurrection interpreted as the immortality of the soul. Although the insertion of these explanations into the Christian story is easily justified, the unfortunate tendency to yoke this story to one philosophical system, namely, Neoplatonic thought, robbed it of its rhetorical elegance and flexibility on the one hand, and laid the groundwork, on the other hand, for the gradual glossing-over of death and the one-sided insistence on immortality and the world of the spirit--the other world.[103]

In any re-telling of the Christian story, then, we would do well to heed the guidelines furnished by our theology of limit. Death as the limit-to life accentuates the elements of limitation, finality, and mortality (mors = death). Death as the limit-of life is expressed metaphorically by the term "resurrection." Whether there need be more than symbolism conveyed by "belief in resurrection" is a hermeneutical question. The interpretation seems to parallel the mind-set of the community interpreting the metaphor. The shift in recent years, it seems, is away from the immortality of the soul as the adequate and appropriate model to express "resurrection" (limit-of death), and toward some kind of altered state of consciousness.[104]

A concluding word is in order about the process of remythicization, that is, the transition from one myth to another through parabolic reversal. It is we, once again, who are reconstructing the current story, and therefore the same rigor demanded by the theology of limit limits our particular constructive theology. It seems closer to the parabolic model of the Parable himself, therefore, to watch settling in on any myth. Yes, the terror of history is removed, but also removed may be the possibility of transcendence. The ultimate parable, death-resurrection, is the basis of faith.

iv. ANALOGY AND THE CONTRIBUTION OF PHILOSOPHY.
Earlier in our essay we developed the theology of limit around the various modes of story.[105] The antithesis

of myth, the palliative, reconciling mode of story, we
noted, is parable, the story that shatters worlds and
subverts myths. Limit, as a theological methodology,
emphasizes the parabolic, reversal mode of story. In
the process, however, a new story emerges Phoenix-like
from the ashes of myth. So far in this part of my
essay I have been remythicizing, or re-constructing
the story. I would like finally to explore the middle
forms of story between myth and parable, namely,
apologue and justification, the explanatory modes of
story. I have been calling this the analogical
dimension of story.

Particularly helpful from the philosophical
models available to the contemporary analogical imagination are Martin Heidegger's "Being-toward-Death" and
Karl Rahner's "All-Cosmic Relationship." We will explore these analogies individually.

a. <u>Heidegger</u> and "<u>Being-toward Death</u>".

> Death is thus a possibility of the being
> of Dasein, a potentiality always before
> and with him, right from the very be-
> ginning of his existence... In the exis-
> tential-ontological sense, this means
> that death belongs to the very constitu-
> tion of man; it is an essential element
> of being of Dasein. In this sense,
> "Death is a way to be, which Dasein takes
> over as soon as it is (<u>SZ</u> 245). In this
> way of thinking death is considered not
> as the brute fact of cessation, or the
> point-like event of coming to an end, for
> this would be an ontic mode of expression.
> Death is an ever-present element in the
> ontological structure of Dasein, a deter-
> mination of existence, which Heidegger
> calls an "existential." The particular
> name of this existential is "being-unto-
> end" or "being-unto-death (<u>SZ</u> 245). [106]

George Steiner describes Heidegger's phrase, "Being-
towards-death" (<u>Sein zum Tode</u>) as "one of the most
often cited, least understood tags in modern
thought."[107] In order to avoid Steiner's accusation,
I think it is helpful to explore three facets of
Heidegger's thought captured by three characteristical-
ly Heideggerian terms: Being-there (Dasein), authen-

ticity, and anticipation of Death.

1. Dasein. Heidegger's description of human existence (or person) is simply "there-Being."[108] This expression grows out of his rejection of the subject-object analysis of human existence, and the dichotomy between the knower and what he knows. In other words, a person is always aware of (it)self as being-in-the-world. To be human is to be immersed, implanted, rooted in the earth. To accentuate this point Heidegger uses the composite "being-in-the-world" (In-der-Welt-Sein). Dasein, or there-being, is clearly not isolated autonomous existence, but is also with-others. This being the case, we come to exist not by ourselves or for ourselves, but in relationship to and in reference to others (das Man). The end result is that in the relationship to the others ("they"), Dasein tends to assimilate itself to the others.[109] This is the point at which Heidegger introduces the key distinction between an authentic and an inauthentic condition of human life.

2. Authentic Existence. Heidegger perceives the two basic possibilities of Dasein's being as being authentic, in a real way, and being inauthentic, that is, being in a way that is untrue.[110]

We should note that it is not as though living inauthentically is something we necessarily choose. Everyone lives inauthentically much of the time, that is, we tend to go along with the crowd, to live as the "they" (others, das Man), to live according to custom and habit. One might draw an interesting parallel between Heidegger's inauthentic existence and Lawrence Kohlberg's conventional morality in the stages of moral development. It is not that persons are necessarily "inauthentic"; rather, their level of moral development is as yet ideally incomplete. The transition from inauthentic to authentic existence involves one in intense and demanding experiences, of which dread (Angst, anxiety) and anticipation of death (Sein zum Tode) are the two dramatic instances.[111] Dread or anxiety is differentiated from fear, since fear is always fear of something, whereas anxiety has no particular object; it represents a feeling of uneasiness about existence itself. Anxiety, as it were, initiates the process of one's questioning the familiar, the realm of everydayness, and moves one gradually from inauthentic to authentic existence. It is the repudiation of "theyness" (others, _das Man_) as the measure of one's existence. The other extreme experience (or limit-experience) is anticipation of death.

3. Anticipation of Death. Even though the most pointed experience of anxiety, dread, or Angst is death itself, Heidegger's "being-towards-death" is not the morbid preoccupation with dying that sometimes overwhelms people.[112] It is rather the courageous confrontation and surrender described by Tolstoy in the death of Ivan Illich, mentioned also by Heidegger in one of his works:

> For three whole days, during which time did not exist for him, he struggled in that black sack into which he was being thrust by an invisible, resistless force. He struggled as a man condemned to death struggles in the hands of the executioner, knowing that he cannot save himself. And every moment he felt that despite all his efforts he was drawing nearer and nearer to what terrified him. He felt that his agony was due to his being thrust into that black hole and still more to his not being able to get right into it. He was hindered from getting into it by his conviction that his life had been a good one. That very justification of his life held him fast and prevented his moving forward, and it caused him most torment of all.
> Suddenly some force struck him in the chest and side, making it still harder to breathe, and he fell through the hole and there at the bottom was a light. What had happened to him was like the sensation one sometimes experiences in a railway carriage when one thinks one is going backwards while one is really going forwards and suddenly becomes aware of the real direction...
> In place of death there was light...[113]

For Heidegger, then, death signifies both the biological reality of end ("being-at-an-end") or limit-to and the ontological experience of potentiality or limit-of. Death is not only the end of life (a future reality); it is also the limit to one's potentiality as a whole (future impinging on the present in relation

158

to the past). This approach, as we suggested earlier, very nearly approximates the dual notion of limit that we have been using throughout this essay: death is both limit-to life (biological termination) and limit-of life (ontological-existential confrontation of finitude and mortality):

> ... The distinction being made is that between the negative mundanity of "fear" and ontologically vital "care" that comes of Angst. Thus an authentic death has to be striven for. A true being-toward-the-end is one which labors consciously toward fulfillment and refuses inertia; it is one which seeks an ontological grasp of its own finitude rather than taking refuge in the banal conventionality of general biological extinction.[114]

It is in the responsible confrontation and acceptance of death (not only biological but ontological death) that one experiences radically and for the first time who he is, Dasein, "there-being," through which disclosure (of Being) occurs. It is only in openness to the mysterious totality of existence (not just "this" or "that" dimension) that this revelation can occur. Heidegger's description is terse and precise: "(Death) as the shrine of Non-Being, hides within itself the presence of Being."[115] Accepting death is the act of opening up to Being.

In conclusion, much of what we have come to describe as the existential approach to death is thoroughly argued and convincingly urged in Heidegger's discussion of Being, man, and death. Given the concreteness of personal existence in the world with others, one struggles from inauthenticity to authenticity, overcoming the humdrum of everyday existence. The most intense experience or anxiety in achieving authenticity is the confrontation with ontological death, the beginning of authentic human existence. This is death as the limit-of life and the disclosure of Being.

2. Rahner and Death as All-Cosmic Relationship. If for Heidegger the study of the limit-nature of death "remains purely 'this-worldly' insofar as it interprets this phenomenon merely in terms of the way it enters into a particular Dasein as a possibility of its

being,"[116] that is not the case for theologians generally, and especially for Roman Catholic theologians. They find it virtually impossible, it would appear, to discuss the reality of death without simultaneously entering into the question about life-after-death, almost in the same sense suggested by Mircea Eliade: "Death is inconceivable if it is not related to a new form of being in some way or other, no matter how this form may be imagined: a post-existence, rebirth, reincarnation, spiritual immortality, or resurrection of the body."[117]

A representative of current philosophizing within the Christian tradition, Karl Rahner takes seriously the so-called existentialist position and especially the contributions of Heidegger to the "new mode" in philosophy.[118] This general orientation leads Rahner to object strenuously to the classic view of death. Although it had important functions in Christian tradtion, this view of death as the separation of body and soul is far from adequate. And this for two reasons principally: first, its failure to speak of death as a personal event that strikes man in his totality, and, second, its disregard for the impact that death has on the person's (soul's?) relationship to the world. Both of these elements are central to Rahner's philosophical contribution to the Christian story of death, and we need to pursue them in some detail.

1. <u>Death</u> <u>as</u> <u>a</u> <u>radically</u> <u>personal</u> <u>event</u>.

> ... It is <u>man</u> that dies: that is, in death something happens to him as a whole, something which, consequently is of essential importance to his soul as well; his free personal self-affirmation and self-realization achieves in death an absolute determination. This determination should not be conceived as something occurring at the moment of death on, after it, or extrinsic to it; it must be considered as an intrinsic element of death itself. But the fact that human death does contain this characteristic element of final decision is not at all indicated by the expression, "separation of body and soul."[119]

Rahner emphasizes in his comments here what we have been calling the limit-to dimension of death: death is the absolute end of the person (as embodied consciousness). In some of the writings of Rahner's Catholic colleagues, death is seen as the moment of final decision. Ladislaus Boros calls death the first truly free, human act of the person.[120] They reject out of hand the rather passive and matter-of-fact description of death merely as the separation of body and soul. Rahner makes the point unequivocally: "If death be the end for the whole man; that is if through death the whole man arrives at the end of his temporal existence, which is characteristic of human life and which finds its termination precisely in death, then this end must have its impact upon the whole man, the soul included..."[121]

We might make the point perhaps that in Rahner's description of death as an event concerning man as a whole, as well as in Boros' final option theory, they have a slightly different approach than Heidegger's "being-towards-death." Heidegger, as we noted earlier, distinguishes between biological and ontological death, and envisions ontological death as the critical moment in life (Sein zum Tode) when one passes from inauthenticity. Rahner (and Boros, for that matter) on the other hand gives the impression that, even though he might go along with the distinction between biological and ontological death, there would be nonetheless chronological simultaneity. One might say, in other words, that for Rahner biological death is the context of ontological death (authenticity and finality). It may be that the underlying assumption of life after death makes the moment of death (biological) critical (ontologically and existentially), since one's fate in relationship to the future life is sealed forever at the moment of death. Heidegger instead fixes his sights on "death as it enters into a particular Dasein as a possibility of its being." It is death as absolute end (biological) which opens one up to possibility, but the possibility is existentiell (in the moment) as well as existential, to use Heidegger's technical distinctions, and ontic as well as ontological.

Although I find Rahner (and Boros) creative in his interpretation of traditional stories about death, I cannot help but judge him in terms of his assumption about afterlife, an assumption which colors his notion of ontological death (death as limit-of human existence) and differentiates him significantly from Heidegger. At the same time, their insights regarding death are definite milestones in Christian philosophical and theological thinking, since they accentuate the finality of death: death as limit-to life. They do not gloss over death out of religious allegiance to resurrection (or philosophical allegiance to immortality of the soul).

2. Death as All-Cosmic Relationship.

> The separation of soul and body is usually conceived to imply, in a rather matter-of-fact way, that the soul becomes a-cosmic. This conception prevails because by instinct--or, so to speak more precisely, under the persistent influence of a Neoplatonic mentality--we tend to assume that the appearance of the soul before God, which, faith teaches us, takes place at death, stands in some direct opposition to their present relationship to the world, as though freedom from matter and nearness to God must increase. When, however, we manage to grasp the metaphysical and religious implications of such uncritically accepted premises... then we will no longer find it impossible to accept death as a separation of body and soul in the second sense, that is, in that which implies an all-cosmic stage of life... in death the soul becomes not a-cosmic but all-cosmic."122

Rahner goes on to caution that his notion of all-cosmic does not imply that the soul is omnipresent to the universe or that the world in some way becomes the "new" body of the soul. What he would seem to be accentuating is that the person lives forever. Person, however, is a relationship between matter and consciousness (psyche, soul). At death that relationship does not cease; otherwise one would have the total destruction (or annihilation) of the person. Rahner insists therefore that the relationship continues, but is changed. It is no longer simply "this" matter (one's body), but universal matter. Just as the soul (spirit, consciousness) was so imbedded here, it will be imbedded in matter hereafter, but that imbeddedness will be pan-cosmic, that is, related to the cosmos as a whole.

I find Rahner's theory of "all-cosmic relationship"

162

a much more imaginative interpretation of "resurrection" than the immortality of the soul. If one must continue to tell a story of resurrection as existence in another world for each and every individual, at least the story of pan-cosmic relatedness accentuates the reality of one's relationship to this world in a way which is much more responsible--socially and ecologically--than the traditional a-cosmic emphasis which led to the renunciation of and disengagement from "building the earth," or bringing the Kingdom into being.

In conclusion, I think that one's assessment of Rahner's contributions to death-as-limit will necessarily be qualified in the final analysis by one's acceptance or rejection of his basic assumption of personal survival after death. Whatever that assessment, Rahner does expand the context of Christian faith, opening up particularly two dimensions of the classic understanding of death. In the categories we have been developing in this essay he accentuates the notion of death both as limit-to life (limiting, finalizing, terminating) and as limit-of life (grounding, challenging, revealing). Rahner emphasizes death as that event which affects the person in his totality. It is not just the separation of body and soul, but the dissolution of the person as that person is known. At the same time he suggests that a new mode of existence for that person--given the survival hypothesis--should be seen not as a-cosmic (which only reinforces all the traditional negativity about matter and earthly existence generally), but rather as all-cosmic. Death may very well be a new and different relationship between consciousness and matter ("a much closer, more intimate relationship to the universe as a whole"), not the necessarily limited relationship possible through this body, but a "deeper, all-embracing openness," an all-cosmic relationship. These are refreshingly new concepts for the metaphysical dimension of the Christian story.

CONCLUSION:

In the concluding part of this essay I have attempted to apply the principles and method of the theology of limit to the human experience of dying and death. With this the trinity of limit-experiences is complete: language, environment, and death.

The primary function of the theology of limit, as
was stressed in the previous two parts, is the obvious
one of accentuating the reality of limits, especially
the limitation of language itself. As story, the
theology of limit parallels paradox and parable; it
challenges, that is, the prevailing myth. In the particular experience discussed here, man and the limits
of mortality, deconstruction and demythicization
proved especially difficult, since the mechanisms of
repression and avoidance are so much a part of the
contemporary (Western) reaction to dying and death.
We discovered, however, that exploration into the approaches of biology, psychology and philosophy lead
inevitably to an awareness of human mortality and
finitude. That fact is unequivocal: at death "I"
cease to be; "my world" comes to an end. Death is the
cessation of embodied consciousness and the end of
the person's world.

The second function of the theology of limit, and
one that more nearly parallels the theology of story-
as-myth, follows directly from the unequivocal affirmation of death as limit-to life. In the face of this
stark realization humans manifest a strong tendency, in
Wittengstein's language, to push and strain at the
limit that death is (limit-of dimension). This
tendency has resulted in three basic attitudes toward
death and three corresponding stories: the myth of
avoidance and repression; the myth of death as prelude
to afterlife (personal survival); and the myth of death
as existential challenge to authenticity. The myth of
avoidance and repression, whether it follows the
Epicurean script (Death is not to be feared, since
while we are it is not, and when it comes we are not),
or Stoic resistance to suffering and death (Christian
Science), the brute fact of mortality and finitude is
repressed. We expanded on this repression/avoidance
posture by highlighting three common cultural themes:
death as pornographic and forbidden; modern funereal
practices; and the particular problems arising within
a scientific and technological society. The second
myth regarding personal encounter with death as limitation is the universal narrative about life after
death. Such stories, notwithstanding their intrinsic
worth and power as myths, tend to shift attention away
from the reality of death as limit-to life. The third
myth about death as finality is the story portraying

death as existential challenge to authentic life.
This myth represents death as opening up to us (or
opening us up to) the authentic possibilities of human
existence. This narrative places less emphasis on the
question of life after death and focuses more on death
as abiding challenge to assess the quality and meaning
of one's life at any given point along the inexorable
movement toward death (biological). In other words,
given that I shall die, how should I live?

A third function of the theology of limit addresses the specific issue of the religious stories
about death and the possibility of re-presenting and
re-telling them. This function in turn has two ob-
jectives: first, to understand the rhetoric of the
narratives themselves, and, secondly, to unpack the
metaphysical assumptions connected with this rhetoric.
Reflecting primarily on the Western, and specifically
Christian, story, we noted that the gradual shift away
from belief in the resurrection of the body (flesh)
and toward belief (or rational assent) in the immortality of the soul created a radically new (mis-)
direction for the story about death and the survival
hypothesis. Any re-telling and re-presenting of that
religious tradition, therefore, would have to be
thought through both in the context of the theology of
limits and in terms of the traditional narrative about
death-resurrection. This primordial dyad fully employs
both dimensions of the theology of limit: death
affirms the limit-to life (immortality, finitude,
termination); resurrection addresses the limit-of life.
Whether "resurrection" need be more than symbolic
("life is worth living--even in the face of death") is
a hermeneutical question. Each generation of
Christians shall have to struggle with the meaning of
"resurrection of the dead" for its time.

Finally, searching out the metaphysical assumptions of the traditional narratives, we offered two
philosophical accounts which strengthen the primordial
myth of death (limit-to life) and resurrection (limit-
of life), namely, Martin Heidegger's "Being-toward
death," and Karl Rahner's "All-cosmic relationahips."
The thrust of Heidegger's thought is toward a
thoroughly argued existential interpretation of death.
His emphasis is on death primarily as the limit-of life,
and its corresponding disclosure of Being. The particularly helpful insight from Rahner, on the other
hand, is that his model of death as "all-cosmic

relationship" represents a much more comprehensive and imaginative interpretation of resurrection (limit-of death) than the traditional theologically adapted "immortality of the soul." And even with his focus on the transformational dimension of death, Rahner continues to emphasize the notion of death as the complete break-up of the person--as we know "person."

In sum, these two philosophical directions lend themselves most readily to the re-description and re-presentation of the traditional Christian story of death-resurrection.

CHAPTER IV NOTES

1. Jorge Luis Borges, _Dreamtigers_. Translated by Mildred Boyer and Harold Morland (New York: Dutton, 1970), p. 91.

2. John Dunne, _Reasons of the Heart_, p. 174.

3. I emphasize the modifier "generally" because the poet seems to bring language and death together in a unique way. See Linda Leonard, "The Belonging together of Poetry and Death."

4. A. R. Ammons, _The Snow Poems_ (New York: Norton, 1977), p. 2.

5. _The Poetry of Yvor Winters_ (Chicago: Swallow Press, 1978), p. 116.

6. Sigmund Freud, "Thoughts for the Times on War and Death," In _On War, Sex and Neurosis_ (New York: Arts & Sciences Press, 1947), p. 263.

7. _Tractatus_, 6.4311. Concerning Wittgenstein's views on death, see William H. Breuning, "Wittgenstein's View of Death," _Philosophical Studies_ (Ireland), 25:1977, pp. 48-68; A. C. Genova, "Death as a Terminus ad Quem," _Philosophy and Phenomenological Research_ 34:1973, pp. 270-77; James W. Van Evra, "On Death as a 'Limit'," _Analysis_ 31:1971, pp. 170-76; Edith Wyschogrod, "Death and Some Philosophies of Language," _Philosophy Today_ 22:1978, pp. 255-65.

8. _Notebooks_, 1914-16 (New York: Harper & Row, 1961), See pp. 72e-753 _passim_. One might raise the hypothetical question of "another language" and "another place." That is not our concern here.

9. _Ibid_.

10. See William Breuning, _art. cit._, p. 66.

11. See above, Part II, 2, iii.

12. _Poems by Emily Dickinson_. Edited by T. W. Higginson and Mabel Loomis Todd (Boston: Roberts Brothers, 1893), p. 201.

13. See Elizabeth Kubler-Ross, On Death and Dying
    (New York: Macmillan, 1969), pp. 11ff. Kubler-
    Ross's work marks a significant step in American
    society from systematic avoidance of death to
    efforts to come to grips with its reality.

14. There is an interesting correlation between lan-
    guage and death. Peter Koestenbaum talks about
    our "inventing death." See Is There An Answer to
    Death? (Englewood Cliffs, NJ: Prentice-Hall,
    Inc., 1976), pp. 84ff.

15. See R. Huntington and P. Metcalf, Celebrations of
    Death: The Anthropology of Mortuary Ritual (New
    York: Cambridge University Press, 1979), pp.
    184ff.

16. This is a curious transition in a society that
    has shifted its emphasis from the Humanities in
    the academic curriculum to the Sciences.
    Interesting also is the switch from fear and
    concern over heart surgery to fear and concern
    over brain surgery.

17. Robert M. Veatch, "Defining Death Anew," in Dying:
    Facing the Facts. Edited by Hannelore Wass (New
    York: McGraw-Hill, 1979), p. 357.

18. Ibid. In this connection Dr. Christiaan Barnard's
    experience is revealing:
        "I'll not lift an instrument until the EKG
        line is flat," said Terry O'Donovan.
        I nodded, knowing how he felt.
        All the years of our training, all the
        structures of our belief rested on one con-
        cept--to protect life, not to take it. Yet
        what life were we protecting in waiting for
        this heart to die--and perhaps injure it-
        self? Certainly not Washansky's. Nor
        could we take away the life of Denise
        Darvall, for it had already been removed
        from her. So this was not another tempta-
        tion to commit the great transgression--to
        cross the line and play God, to decide when
        a life should be terminated. Here there
        was no decision to be made by us. It had
        already been made. Denise Darvall was be-
        yond the possibility of living. Clinically,
        she was dead. Her heart lived on, yes--but
        it had been supported by us, to reach this

moment when we could take it to a man
waiting in another room.
"What do you say, Chris?"
Marius spoke as though he knew my
thoughts--and believed we should take the
heart now.
"No, we must wait until it stops."
Christiaan Barnard and Curtis Bill Pepper,
Christiaan Barnard, One Life (New York: Mac-
millan, 1969), pp. 59-60.

19. The Collected Poems of Theodore Roethke, p. 4.

20. In keeping with my earlier suggestion about sus-
pending belief regarding after death issues, I
emphasize the focus here: the nature of death.

21. From "The Palace," In The Gold of the Tigers.
Translated by Alastair Reid (New York: Dutton,
1977), p. 39.

22. See Gary Jones, "Death and After Death," Journal
of Medicine and Philosophy 4:1979, pp. 234-237.
Cf. p. 236.

23. For a working distinction between "loss" and
"absence," see G. Jones, art. cit., p. 235.

24. A. C. Genova's comments are pointed: " ... The
most significant feature of the human experiential context... is found in the fact of self-
consciousness... human beings are presumably the
only beings who fully know of their impending
death--of the irrevocable fact that all their
projects, hopes and experiences will one day be
permanently terminated... " (p. 276).

25. There are various psychological exercises in
fantasizing death and one's own experience of
death. See, for example, Robert E. Neale, The
Art of Dying, pp. 2, 3, 5, 9, and passim, and
Peter Koestenbaum, op. cit., pp. 188ff.

26. I caution again that I am making no judgment here
about any other kind of "I," ego," or "self";
only the embodied, earthly self.

27. See Colleen Clements, "Death and Philosophical
Diversions," Philosophy & Phenomenological Research 39:1978, pp. 524-36.

28. See A. C. Genova, "Death as a <u>Terminus</u> <u>ad</u> <u>Quem</u>," for an interesting discussion of the contemporary expression of that philosophy.

29. Colleen Clements, <u>art</u>. <u>cit</u>., p. 529.

30. Edith Wyschogrod, <u>art</u>. <u>cit</u>., p. 255.

31. <u>Tractatus</u> 6.431 and 6.4311.

32. See above, note 7.

33. <u>Tractatus</u> 5.6.

34. "Wittgenstein's Lecture on Ethics," <u>Philosophy Review</u> 74:1965, pp. 13-16.

35. See Ludwig Wittgenstein, <u>Notebooks,1914-16</u>, p. 73.

36. William Breuning, "Wittgenstein's View of Death," p. 73.

37. Yevgeny Yevtushenko, from his "People" in <u>Selected Poems</u>. Translated with an introduction by Robin Milner-Gulland and Peter Levi (New York: E. P. Dutton & Co., 1962), p. 85.

38. Stewart Alsop, <u>Stay of Execution</u>. Cited in <u>Death in Literature</u>, p. 98.

39. <u>The Poetry of Yvor Winters</u>, p. 185.

40. Frederick Morgan, <u>Death Mother and Other Poems</u> (Chicago: University of Illinois Press, 1979), p. 4.

41. See Mircea Eliade, "Mythologies of Death: An Introduction," in <u>Religious Encounter With Death</u>. Edited by F. Reynolds & E. Waugh (University Park, PA: Pennsylvania State University Press, 1977), p. 13.

42. It appears the Tasaday (Stone Age Group) attitude toward death is similar. See Colleen Clements, <u>art</u>. <u>cit</u>., p. 530.

43. No attempt will be made here to furnish anything but a minimal bibliography. Some of the classics in the field are: Phillipe Aries, Western Attitudes Towards Death (Baltimore: Johns Hopkins U. Press, 1974); Ernest Becker, The Denial of Death (New York: Free Press, 1973); Jacques Choron, Death and Western Thought (New York: Collier Books, 1963); Herman Feifel (ed.), The Meaning of Death (New York: McGraw-Hill, 1959); B. G. Glaser and A. L. Strauss, Awareness of Dying (Chicago: Aldine Press, 1965); Geoffrey Gorer, Death, Grief and Mourning (Garden City, NY: Doubleday, Inc., 1965); Elizabeth Kubler-Ross, On Death and Dying (New York: Macmillan Publishing Co., 1969); Arien Mack (ed.), Death in American Experience (New York: Schocken Books, 1973); Jessica Mitford, The American Way of Death (New York: Simon and Schuster, 1963); A. D. Weisman, On Dying and Denying: A Psychiatric Study of Terminality (New York: Behavioral Publications, 1973).

Among more recent anthologies are: Edwin S. Schneidman (ed.), Death: Current Perspectives (Palo Alto, CA: Mayfield Publishing Company, 1980); Hannelore Wass (ed.), Dying: Facing the Facts (New York: Hemisphere, 1979); S. G Wilcox and M. Sutter, Understanding Death and Dying: An Interdisciplinary Approach (Port Washington, NY: Alfred Publishing Co., 1977).

44. Geoffrey Gorer, Death, Grief and Mourning.

45. Phillipe Aries, Western Attitudes Towards Death.

46. G. Gorer, p. 195.

47. See Wendell Stacy Johnson, Living in Sin: The Victorian Sexual Revolution (Chicago: Nelson-Hall, 1979).

48. See Robert E. Neale, The Art of Dying, p. 8.

49. Quoted in Robert E. Neale, p. 7.

50. Collected Earlier Poems (New York: New Directions, 1938), pp. 129-31. Theodore Roethke adds another perspective in his On the Road to Woodlawn:

> I miss the polished brass, the powerful
>   black horses,
> The drivers creaking the seats of the baroque hearses,
> The high-piled floral offering with sentimental verses,
> The carriage reeking with varnish and stale
>   perfume.
>
> I miss the pallbearers momentously taking
>   their places,
> The undertaker's obsequious grimaces,
> The craned necks, the mourners' anonymous
>   faces,
> --And the eyes, still vivid, looking up
>   from a sunken room.

The Collected Poems of Theodore Roethke, p. 4.

51. The title of Jessica Mitford's pioneering study on death.

52. See Linda Leonard, "The Belonging-Together of Poetry and Death," p. 139.

53. See Eric Cassell, "Being and Becoming Dead," in Death in American Experience, p. 166.

54. See Elizabeth Kubler-Ross, On Death and Dying, p. 22ff.

55. See Mircea Eliade, "Mythologies of Death," p. 13.

56. Cited earlier, p. 117, n. 6.

57. There is an interesting play on words that is currently going on. We have been accustomed to speak of "afterlife," or "life after death." "Life after life" and "After-death" are the new (paradoxical) phrases.

58. Perhaps one need not adopt the raw-boned approach of John Dominic Crossan's "Immortality as Idolatry: The Limits of Narcotic Theology," Listening 10:1975, pp. 21-29. I think, however, that more and more the story of afterlife (in whatever form) is being re-thought--if not totally revoked.

59. Cited in Rollo May, Love and Will (New York: W. W. Norton, 1969), p. 99.

60. Linda Leonard, art. cit., p. 139.

61. William Breuning, art. cit., pp. 66f. The italics are mine.

62. Rainer Maria Rilke, Duino Elegies and The Sonnets to Orpheus. Translated by A. Poulin, Jr. (Boston: Houghton Mifflin Co., 1977), p. 101.

63. Cornelius Ryan and Kathryn Morgan Ryan, A Private Battle (New York: Simon and Schuster, 1979). Cited in Death in Literature, pp. 106f.

64. Sam Keen, "The Heroics of Everyday Life: A Theorist of Death Confronts His Own End," Psychology Today, April, 1974, pp. 71-80. The parenthesis in the quote is from a previous paragraph in the interview, p. 78.

65. Colleen Clements, art. cit., p. 533.

66. T. S. Eliot, The Complete Poems and Plays, 1909-1950 (New York: Harcourt, Brace and Co., 1952), p. 126.

67. Colleen Clements, art. cit., p. 531.

68. Sam Keen, art. cit., p. 71.

69. See Robert Neale, The Art of Dying, p. 13, of which this is a paraphrase.

70. The Poetry of Yvor Winters, p. 134.

71. Tao Teh Ching, #16. Introduction and Commentary by K. O. Schmidt (Lakemont, GA: CSA Press, 1975), p. 77.

72. See ahead, note 87 for the bibliographic references.

73. Mircea, Eliade, loc. cit., p. 15.

74. Ibid., p. 16.

75. As Eliade Notes: "... It is well known among traditional societies that death is not considered real until the funerary ceremonies are duly completed. In other words, the onset of physiological death is only the signal that a new set of ritual operations must be accomplished in order to create the new identity of the deceased. The body has to be treated in such a way that it will not be magically reanimated and become an instrument of mischievous performances. Even more important, the soul must be guided to her new abode and ritually integrated in the community of its inhabitants." Loc. cit., p. 15.

76. Again Eliade's comments are incisive: "... Death is inconceivable if it is not related to a new form of being in some way or other, no matter how this form may be imagined..." Loc. cit., p. 21.

77. John Dominic Crossan, "Immortality as Idolatry.. ..," pp. 28f. John Fowles has an equally direct approach in his The Aristos (New York: New American Librayr, 1970): "... We stand at this great insight now: there is no life after death. Soon this will be as certain to everyone as it is certain to me, where I write, that there is no one in the next room. It is true that I cannot absolutely prove there is no one without going into the room; but all the circumstantial evidence supports my belief. Death is the room that is always empty.
    "The great linked myths of the afterlife and the immortal soul have served their purpose; have stood between us and reality. But their going will change all, and is meant to change all." Pp. 38-9.

78. Robert E. Neale, The Art of Dying, p. 13.

79. Complete Poems of Robert Frost (New York: Henry Holt, 1949), p. 540.

80. See earlier, Part III, i., b.

81. See my article in New Catholic Encyclopedia v. "Resurrection of the Dead, 2. Theology of," vol. 12, pp. 424-427.

82. The Hindu principle of Maya is somewhat similar. The reality, however, is not of another world, but an intense experience of this world. See Huston Smith, The Religions of Man, pp. 82-85.

83. Walt Whitman, Leaves of Grass (Mount Vernon, NY: Peter Pauper Press, 1943), p. 236.

84. Very early in its history the Christian profession of faith in resurrection of the body encountered the Neo-platonic notion of the body/soul distinction, and found it helpful to explain the interim between death and general resurrection.

85. God's Trombones (New York: Viking Press, 1927), p. 27.

86. All the while, of course, one is mindful of Jesus' experience of death and its physical and psychological demands on him.

87. Following is a very basic philosophy on death in the religions of the world: S. G. F. Brandon, The Judgement of the Dead: The Idea of Life After Death In the Major Religions (New York: Charles Scribner's Sons, 1967); Frederick H. Holt (ed.), Death and Eastern Thought (Nashville: Abingdon, 1974); Christopher C. Hong, Eschatology of the World Religions (Washington, DC: University Press of America, 1976); F. E. Reynolds and E. Waugh, Religious Encounter With Death.

88. See especially S. G. F. Brandon, The Judgement of the Dead, pp. 5; 193-95.

89. Chuang Tzu, "Perfect Happiness." Cited in Frederick Holt, Death and Eastern Thought, p. 222.

90. See Phillippe Aries (<u>Western Attitudes Towards
    Death</u>): "Death was a ritual organized by the
    dying person himself, who presided over it and
    knew its protocol... It was essential that
    parents, friends, and neighbors be present.
    Children were brought in; until the eighteenth
    century no portrayal of a deathbed scene failed
    to include children. And to think of how care-
    fully people today keep children away from any-
    thing having to do with death!" (pp. 11f.).
        I do not wish here to disregard the seeming
    natural tendency within man to long for the
    eternal (Freud, etc.), but simply to emphasize
    the clear and direct experience of death in
    earlier societies.

91. <u>Poems of Emily Dickinson</u>. Selected by Helen
    Plotz (New York: Thomas Crowell Co., 1964).
    Karen Mills Campbell in an article, "Poetry as
    Epitaph," <u>Journal of Popular Culture</u> 14:1981,
    657-668, has an interesting study of immortality
    in Emily Dickinson's poetry: "Her Christian soul
    never surrendered the possibility of heavenly
    mortality. Yet her fine poet's mind never sur-
    rendered the hope that her words would continue
    to exist in 'Earths to come'..." (p. 667).

92. Cited in William Breuning, "Wittgenstein's View
    of Death," p. 67, n. 15.

93. Mircea Eliade, <u>loc</u>. <u>cit</u>., p. 20.

94. Cited in Edwin S. Schneidman, <u>Death: Current
    Perspectives</u>, p. 533f.

95. See above, Part II, iv., a.

96. The question of the survival of the individual in
    Jewish Scriptures is a complex question. See
    Wolfram Hermann, "Human Mortality as a Problem in
    Ancient Israel," In Reynolds and Waugh, <u>Religious
    Encounter With Death</u>, pp. 159-69.

97. Authors tend to distinguish between "historical"
    and "metaphorical and mythic." John Dominic
    Crossan has a provocative comment: "People are
    fond of discussing two types of religion, his-
    torical and mythical, and of asserting that
    Judaism and Christianity are in the former

category because they link their claims to the objective reality of certain key events. Maybe the time has come to retire this distinction as irrelevant and to replace it with another. The more useful distinction might be between mythical religion, a religion that gives one the final word about 'reality' and thereby excludes the authentic experience of mystery, and parabolic religion, a religion that continually and deliberately subverts final words about 'reality' and thereby introduces the possibility of transcendence." The Dark Interval, pp. 127-28.

98. See Christopher C. Hong, Eschatology of the World Religions, pp. 76-79.

99. See my article cited above, n. 81.

100. Norman Perrin, New Testament: Introduction (New York: Harcourt Brace Jovanovich, 1974), p. 290.

101. The Dark Interval, pp. 124-26.

102. Christianity thus conforms to the general direction of all major world religions. See Eliade, loc. cit.

103. One could continue developing the remaining dimensions of this story: Particular Judgment, Purgatory, Heaven (Beatific Vision), Hell (poena damni, poena sensus), etc.

104. See Morton Kelsey, Afterlife: The Other Side of Dying (New York: Paulist Press, 1979), p. 133. "This is particularly true since the research in parapsychology has begun to provide evidence which seems to support many of the ideas about life after death which have come from the experience and the thinking of believers around the world. Humankind may not have been practicing self-deception after all in believing in another life. There are as many good reasons for believing this as for doubting it. No, there are better reasons for believing in survival after death than for doubting it... "

105. See earlier, Part II, 2, iv., a.

106. William Richardson, Heidegger: Through Phenomenology to Thought (Hague: Martinus Nijhoff,
1967), p. 84.

107. George Steiner, Martin Heidegger, pp. 102f.

108. This is William Richardson's translation of
Dasein.

109. One is reminded of Sartre's l'autre.

110. I am paraphrasing Joan Stambaugh's "A Heidegger
Primer," Philosophy Today 19: 1975, pp. 81f.

111. Another significant instance is the relationship
between Rede (authentic speech) and Gerede
("gossip").

112. Paul Tillich makes an interesting point in The
Courage To Be (New Haven: Yale University Press,
1952): "It is impossible for a finite being to
stand naked anxiety for more than a flash of
time. People who have experienced these
moments... have told of the unimaginable horror
of it." (p. 39).

113. Death of Ivan Illich. Cited in Death in Literature, pp. 438-439.

114. George Steiner, op. cit., p. 105.

115. Cited in Richardson, op. cit., p. 573.

116. Sein und Zeit, 248.

117. Eliade, op. cit., pp. 19f. And yet Gregory Baum
can write in An American Catechism: "To believe
in eternal life cannot be equated with acknow-
ledging the doctrine of the world to come. For
it is possible not to affirm belief in the world
to come, and yet to be carried by a confident
faith that whatever we are, whatever the crisis
we have to face, whatever destruction threatens
us, God's victorious grace will accompany us and
will forever create new life out of our shattered
ruins... " Chicago Studies 12: 1973, p. 311.

118. See Karl Rahner, On the Theology of Death (New York: Herder and Herder, 1961), and "On the Life of the Dead," Theological Investigations, IV (Baltimore: Helicon, 1966).

119. Karl Rahner, On the Theology of Death, pp. 25f.

120. See Ladislaus Boros, The Mystery of Death (New York: Herder and Herder, 1965): "Death is a man's first completely personal act, and is, therefore, by reason of its very being, the place above all others for the awakening of consciousness, for freedom, for the encounter with God, for the final decision about eternal destiny." (p. 84)

121. Karl Rahner, op. cit., pp. 38f.

122. Ibid., pp. 27f.